Praise for *The Awakened Way*

"This former naval officer helps others to come to know the deep truth of connections with a unified spiritual force in the universe that she first encountered on losing her pregnant stepdaughter to a lightning strike—a practical resource for many who are seeking a richer connection with lost loved ones and the spiritual realm in general."

— **Eben Alexander, M.D.**, former Harvard neurosurgeon and author of *Proof of Heaven*, *The Map of Heaven*, and *Living in a Mindful Universe*

"The Awakened Way is not merely another 'self-help' book, but a myriad of spiritual treasures to assist you in remembering that part of your being, which is the holiest of holies, your SOUL. Part manual, part assessment, this transformative compendium will forever shift your perception of what it truly means to be a living soul existing in a human world."

— **James Van Praagh**, spiritual medium and *New York Times* best-selling author

"I am a huge fan of Suzanne Giesemann's work, and I'm delighted with her book The Awakened Way. *There is such promise in these powerful pages as they offer practical how-to's for connecting with our already-present wholeness, making the shift to a divinely guided life, and leaving emptiness and despair behind. Supported by a host of evidential stories of our spiritual nature, this is an inspired guidebook for living in a state of lasting happiness."*

— **Marci Shimoff**, #1 *New York Times* best-selling author of *Happy for No Reason* and *Chicken Soup for the Woman's Soul*

"Embracing The Awakened Way *reveals love as the driving force for creation and healing. Suzanne guides you through exercises that unlock the power within, unveiling your soul's fullness and allowing the expression of your authentic self. Harmonizing with the Universal flow of love, it transforms you into a radiant beacon within the tapestry of existence. A must-read!"*

— **Anita Moorjani**, *New York Times* best-selling author of *Dying to Be Me*, *What if This Is Heaven*, and *Sensitive Is the New Strong*

"Some books are destined to become classics. They educate and inspire us, challenge and guide us, and sometimes integrate and heal us. Suzanne Giesemann's The Awakened Way: Making the Shift to a Divinely Guided Life, does all of this and more. This book combines real-life evidence with personal messages that celebrate the gift of being human. As an academic scientist who has conducted laboratory and field research with mediums and healers for over twenty years in my Laboratory for Advances in Consciousness and Health, I have had the privilege to investigate and validate Suzanne's extraordinary gifts. I have witnessed her growth from being an exceptional evidence-based medium to becoming an awakened spiritual channeler and teacher. This is a book for everyone—from beginning seekers to advanced explorers—and it is ready to read again and again."

— **Gary E. Schwartz**, **Ph.D.**, professor of psychology, medicine, neurology, psychiatry, and surgery at the University of Arizona, author of *The Afterlife Experiments* and *The G.O.D. Experiments*

"Over the years, Suzanne Giesemann has captured the hearts of spiritual practitioners. She has an amazing gift of sharing complex spiritual topics. Suzanne now gifts us with The Awakened Way, showing readers how to avoid the trap of looking for answers outside of oneself. This book contains gems and treasures so needed right now, including practices that will transform your life. It will empower you and show you how to live a life filled with passion and completely transform your perspective on who you have been and who you can become."

— **Sandra Ingerman**, **M.A.**, renowned shamanic teacher and award-winning author of 13 books including *Walking Through Darkness* and *Soul Retrieval*

"Suzanne Giesemann's new book, The Awakened Way, is a down-to-earth guide to moving from feeling disconnected and alone to experiencing your true nature as part of an interconnected family of souls in a benevolent universe. It asks you to consider ways of looking at yourself that are very different from what you have always accepted. I know of no other book comparable to The Awakened Way, which offers not only step-by-step practices to expand your state of awareness, but also ways to validate that these interactive connections are not your imagination."

— **Bruce Greyson**, **M.D.**, professor emeritus of psychiatry and neurobehavioral sciences at the University of Virginia, and author of *After*

"The Awakened Way invites readers to explore that shimmering realm that links human existence with spiritual awareness. Suzanne Giesemann guides us through the process of realizing our true nature, providing practical advice on how to live a more profoundly meaningful and deeply fulfilling life. This book is an invaluable resource for anyone seeking to transcend the mundane BS we are all immersed in (Giesemann's clever shorthand for belief system), and to navigate life's challenges with renewed grace and purpose."

— **Dean Radin, Ph.D.**, chief scientist, Institute of Noetic Sciences, and author of *Real Magic*

"Suzanne Giesemann's The Awakened Way: Making the Shift to a Divinely Guided Life has changed how I view and live my life. As a fellow naval officer who served three sitting American presidents as their physician, my reputation has been that of a woman of 'science' who based her decisions for many years on proof, facts, and data. Suzanne's personal journey and teachings have shown me there is a different perspective that goes BEYOND what we see in the material world. The 'SHIFT' to seeing the world through the eyes of the soul has brought great meaning, purpose, and joy to my life."

— **E. Connie Mariano, M.D.**, Rear Admiral, U.S. Navy (retired) and White House physician (1992–2001), author of *The White House Doctor: My Patients Were Presidents*

"Suzanne Giesemann's newest book, The Awakened Way, *is a powerful volume of knowledge that helps expand the reader's consciousness. Her words will hold your attention and offer you the necessary tools to have your own spiritual awakening—again and again. It is rare to find a book that one desires to read many times over while feeling spirit working through them.* The Awakened Way *is such a book."*

— **Marie Manuchehri, R.N.**, author of *Intuitive Self-Healing* and *How to Communicate with Your Spirit Guides*

"Suzanne Giesemann, a world-renowned medium, has now become one of the West's most gifted spiritual teachers. In her latest book, The Awakened Way, *she offers a distillation of her most important spiritual teachings and perspective. By sharing some of her inspiring stories and keen insights about our true nature, she helps us to become aware that we are more than human beings, but souls whose higher selves serve to transcend our merely human limitations.* The Awakened Way *is, in short, a manual for Self-Realization. Read it and wake up!"*

— **Kenneth Ring, Ph.D.**, author of *Lessons from the Light*

THE AWAKENED WAY

THE AWAKENED WAY

MAKING THE SHIFT TO A DIVINELY GUIDED LIFE

SUZANNE GIESEMANN

HAY HOUSE

Carlsbad, California • New York City
London • Sydney • New Delhi

Published in the United Kingdom by:
Hay House UK Ltd, The Sixth Floor, Watson House
54 Baker Street, London W1U 7BU
Tel: +44 (0)20 3927 7290; www.hayhouse.co.uk

Published in the United States of America by:
Hay House LLC, PO Box 5100, Carlsbad, CA 92018-5100
Tel: (1) 760 431 7695 or (800) 654 5126; www.hayhouse.com

Published in Australia by:
Hay House Australia Publishing Pty Ltd, 18/36 Ralph St, Alexandria
NSW 2015
Tel: (61) 2 9669 4299; www.hayhouse.com.au

Published in India by:
Hay House Publishers India, Muskaan Complex,
Plot No.3, B-2, Vasant Kunj, New Delhi 110 070
Tel: (91) 11 4176 1620; www.hayhouse.co.in

A catalogue record for this book is available from the British Library.

Tradepaper ISBN: 978-1-83782-277-5
E-book ISBN: 978-1-4019-7844-0
Audiobook ISBN: 978-1-4019-7845-7

Cover design: Barbara LeVan Fisher
Interior design: Aaron Robertson
Interior photos: Courtesy of Mike and Beth Pasakarnis

This product uses responsibly sources papers and/or recycled materials.
For more information, see www.hayhouse.co.uk.

Printed and bound by CPI (UK) Ltd, Croydon CR0 4YY

To the love of my life, Ty.
You were part of The Divine Plan all along.

CONTENTS

INTRODUCTION

Heaven on earth.

You may recall enjoying this state at a moment in your life when all seemed right with the world. Perhaps you were with someone you loved in an amazing setting. Regardless of the circumstances, you experienced a sense of completeness and connection with everything and everyone around you. Nothing was missing.

And then, something shifted, and you were back to the *real* world.

That's life, right? What goes up eventually comes back down. Everything is temporary. This can be a blessing if you can't wait for something to end, or it can cause suffering when you become deeply attached to the situations and people in your life.

It isn't easy being human. The one constant is change. Jobs and money come and go. Relationships end. Bodies break down. People you love die.

So, why don't you give up when life becomes too challenging?

You keep going because deep inside is a *knowing* that there is more than this. You move forward one step at a time because beneath the messiness of being human, you sense something good and worth living for.

And you're right. Even though your human side might disagree, there is a part of you that knows you are here for a reason and that life has meaning. There is a spark of awareness that despite what anyone has said to the contrary, you are a bright, shiny being who came here for the fullness of experience in a body.

That part of you is the soul. This spacious state of awareness that knows you are lovable and deserving of joy is not separate from you in any way. It is right here, right now, and it acknowledges with no sense of pride or shame that you are magnificent.

If your initial response to this statement is scorn instead of celebration, don't worry. You're not alone. You have simply bought into the human BS.

That's right: the human *belief system*.

The unquestioning acceptance by most people of the collective fiction that we are only human keeps heaven on earth at a distance. It turns mature adults into fearful, attention-seeking children who make poor choices. It leads to rocky relationships, toxic work environments, and unbalanced bodies. It results in the lingering sense that something is missing. It catapults us into a pit of despair, thinking we are "dead and gone" when the heart stops beating.

Such a belief system can turn your life into a living hell.

If you doubt this, see if any of the following symptoms of believing you are only human hit a bit close to home:

- You don't like silence and fill it with music, television, or talking.

- You turn to excessive sweets, alcohol, drugs, shopping, or other activities to feel better, even when you know they're not good for you.

- You snap easily, often overreact, or experience moments of inexplicable anger.

- You run from others' charged emotions.

- You feel shame, guilt, or unworthiness, despite others' reassurances.

- You often feel an undercurrent of dissatisfaction, no matter how good things seem.

- You are easily affected by others' comments about you.

- You need others' approval to feel good about yourself.

- You compare yourself to others and often feel you don't measure up.

- When people say something nice about you, you brush it off or deny it.

- You have been in one or more dysfunctional relationships.

- You become anxious if you can't check e-mails, texts, or social media regularly.

- You live with a constant fear of death.

- There are times you wish you could join your loved ones who have passed.

If you identify with any of these behaviors, don't worry. Your human side is showing.

Proof that you are not alone in addictive, self-destructive tendencies is visible in every public venue. Look around and what do you see? People standing with their hands clasped and their head bowed. They are not absorbed in prayer. They are worshipping their smartphones.

Why do you panic when you can't find your phone? Because it offers the connection all humans crave. It holds the potential to fill the underlying feeling of emptiness that never seems to go away.

Now hear this! At the human level, you may be wounded and hurting, but at your deepest, most essential level, you are whole and complete. This is because you are not only human. You are also a soul, and your soul is perfectly fine.

You seek connection because your true state is one of undivided wholeness. Problems occur when you look outside yourself to find this wholeness, because the fullness you seek is right here, as close as your breath.

MY WAKE-UP CALL

I was thoroughly caught up in the human BS for much of my life. I used to put a check mark next to most of the dysfunctional behaviors on the list above. And yet, somehow, I enjoyed tremendous success in my career as a naval officer. I served as the commanding officer of a shore unit and as a special assistant to the chief of naval operations. During my final assignment, I was the aide de camp to the head of the U.S. military, the chairman of the joint chiefs of staff.

On the outside, I had my act together, flying on *Air Force One* with the President, meeting kings and queens, and sitting in on top-secret hearings with members of Congress. I retired after 20 years of service with multiple medals and many accolades.

As you may know firsthand, success on the outside does not equate to satisfaction on the inside. I was raised by parents who did not allow my siblings or me to express anything other than positive emotions. "You're not sick!" was a common declaration when any of us didn't feel good.

I didn't know what to do when fear, anger, shame, or guilt welled up inside. Consequently, I became a real pro at stuffing down normal but forbidden emotions. When you put a lid on a simmering pot, the pressure builds. The result for me was an inner battle with overeating that lasted for decades. Today, food no longer controls me—an accomplishment that seemed far from my reach when I had no healthy coping tools.

In the Navy, I steamed full speed ahead through tough times by doing what we were trained to do: I "sucked it up."

That seemed to work just fine until a group of 19 terrorists attacked the World Trade Center and my office building, the Pentagon.

I was the chairman's aide that day, and we were on our way to Europe, where later that week Queen Elizabeth was going to knight my boss. Midway across the Atlantic, we learned of the terrorist attack on our country, and we turned around.

Our flight path took us directly over Manhattan. I thought I was doing a pretty good job of "sucking it up" from inside the last aircraft in U.S. airspace. I gazed down at the smoldering World Trade Center and kept my emotions in check.

We continued to Washington, DC, flanked by Air Force fighter jets. Arriving at the Pentagon, I stepped over pieces of the hijacked aircraft's engine in the grass. I then stood silently, staring at the gaping hole in the building and ignoring the aching hole in my heart.

I felt utterly human and immensely vulnerable thinking of so many lives lost in an instant, but I did not allow myself to show it. I earned an A+ in keeping my composure that first week after 9/11. And then, I was tasked to escort some of the family members of those killed in the attack to a special memorial service for their loved ones. Standing in the presence of such raw grief with no pressure release valve left me physically and emotionally spent.

In the weeks that followed, I couldn't walk the halls of the Pentagon without noticing reminders of the fragility of life. I decided that I would complete my military service on the day I was eligible for retirement and not stay even one day longer. My plans came together perfectly, and I never looked back.

Within 24 hours after leaving the Navy, I sailed into the sunset with my beloved husband, Ty, on our 46-foot sloop. Yes, we were fulfilling a long-held dream of being full-time sailboat cruisers, but in truth, I was also running away from life.

To be sure, this was an idyllic time. We explored and enjoyed the East Coast of the U.S. and Canada and the Bahamas for two years. We achieved a major goal of sailing across the Atlantic Ocean and spent 18 magical months cruising the Mediterranean Sea.

And then, life caught up with us and pulled our sea legs out from under us.

While sailing off the coast of Croatia, we received the devastating news that my stepdaughter, Susan—Ty's beloved youngest daughter—was *"gone."*

That is the word our son-in-law uttered through the phone.

Gone where? was the first thought that entered my mind, even though there was a part of me that knew what he meant. The truth was impossible to face, however, so I held my breath. His explanation shattered my wishful thinking.

He told us that Susan, a sergeant in the U.S. Marine Corps, had been crossing the flight line by her squadron's hangar to report for duty. Suddenly, a bolt of lightning streaked down from the clear blue sky and struck her. Susan was six months pregnant with her first child. Medics worked on her for seven hours, but they could not save Susan or her baby, Liam Tyler.

Unlike in the aftermath of 9/11, I couldn't sail away from this pain or suck it up. Gazing at Susan's lifeless body in the coffin was the most gut-wrenching moment of my life. It was also the most transformational.

Susan's body before me held so little resemblance to the vibrant woman we loved so dearly that I blinked with surprise. Through the haze of grief, I realized that what we call a "person" is far more than physical and cannot be killed. I had no doubt in that pivotal moment that the body is merely a vessel for the immortal Presence that enlivens each of us.

This epiphany surpassed the human intellect that I had relied upon to rise through the ranks in the military. It disarmed all defenses and aroused within my heart an undeniable *knowing* that death is not the end of life.

I knew that the person we had referred to for 27 years as "Susan" was, like each of us, a brightly shining, magnificent soul who came to this earth to be a source of love and joy.

And I knew that if I had any hope of connecting with Susan in her new form, I needed to start meditating. I don't know why I felt that meditation would help. I had never studied or practiced sitting in the silence, yet suddenly, the way ahead was clear.

I became a woman on a mission. I began sitting quietly each morning, asking Susan to make her presence known to me. I had no idea that in doing so, I had embarked on a path that would lead my life in a completely new direction.

I ultimately did connect with Susan. At first, the tearful reunion came via a medium who knew nothing about our family's loss. Unaware of our name or any identifying details, the medium described a woman in her 20s who had died rather suddenly standing before us in a brown uniform. More undeniable validations followed, including the stunning declaration that Susan had brought with her from the spirit world a little baby boy whom she wanted to introduce to us.

That session with a medium rocked my worldview. I walked around in a daze for days. *You mean Susan isn't really dead? There really is a nonphysical world?* I struggled to mesh these undeniable realizations with my long-held human beliefs.

One memorable morning sometime later, while sitting in meditation, I finally achieved my goal. I heard Susan's distinct voice.

"Hey, Suzanne!" she said casually, as if she'd simply been off on a little journey. She then filled my head with greetings for her father and the rest of the family. In response to my request for proof to show that this wondrous visit was not my imagination, she told me three specific things about her biological mother that I had no way of knowing.

Susan reported that her mother's cat was sick, that in the last two days her mother had been looking for a ladder, and that she had Christmas lights strung inside her house year-round. Ty's ex-wife later validated each of these unusual pieces of evidence. This was the first of many visits that left no doubt in our hearts and minds that Susan is still very much a part of our lives.

From that day forward, I worked diligently to hone my ability to communicate not only with Susan but also others who have passed. I recognized this work as my soul's calling. Gratefully, I have been able to pay forward countless times the gift of healing given to our family by the medium who initially brought through Susan so clearly.

My conversations across the veil today extend beyond those who once walked in physical form to what we call angels and master teachers. Since 2010, these wise beings have taught me through daily messages and lengthy channeled sessions about the true reality from which each of us arises.

The teachings include insights that have passed the test of time. They speak to the continuity of consciousness beyond the body. They ring true because they speak to the deepest part of us: the soul.

In my previous career, I had the honor of serving my country at the highest level. I also experienced the depths of human despair, and I found a way out of it that I never imagined when I wore a military uniform. What has convinced me beyond any doubt that you and I are souls temporarily in a physical body is the overwhelming evidence from a greater reality that cannot be known through the limited physical senses.

I know what it's like to feel fully human . . . to feel empty, lost, and desperate. And today, there are times when I am filled with so much joy and love that it tends to overflow. It would be my greatest honor to guide you to higher levels of consciousness so that you, too, will experience the peace and joy that are your birthright.

YOU ARE MAGNIFICENCE

In the years since I embarked on my journey as a spiritual teacher, I have led thousands to awaken to their true nature and transform their lives. To help you see the potential for healing that the teaching and tools in this book promise, please allow me to tell you about my prize pupil to date.

Brenda Bollmann Baker was a teacher and school administrator in her early 60s when we met. As she approached retirement, she inexplicably developed an obsession to learn everything she could about the afterlife. When she saw an announcement that I would be giving a presentation at her local Unity church, she announced to her partner, "We're going!"

I had not yet met Brenda in 2015 when she sat in that Phoenix, Arizona, audience. I did not recognize her when she fled from the church like a frightened deer as soon as my presentation concluded.

I received an e-mail two days later from Brenda via my website. She apologized for intruding and explained that she had never written to an author to share a personal experience. She felt compelled to reach out due to the overwhelming emotions she was experiencing after having attended my "Heart Gifts" presentation.

It seems my talk was aptly named. Its gift to Brenda was the shattering of the well-armored wall she had spent a lifetime carefully erecting around her heart. Sitting in that church, for the first time in her life she felt seen. Unfortunately, that was the last thing she wanted.

Brenda was a large woman with a personality to match. To her friends and colleagues, she came across as bold, brassy, and sassy. This was all a ruse, she explained in her e-mail, camouflaging the ever-present fear that someone might see what she saw when she looked in the mirror. She called it "the ugly."

Her inner battle began in her childhood. Despite being an outstanding student, her parents prized physical appearance above all else. Her father, a respected minister, preached love, yet Brenda faced nothing but rejection and derision from her parents throughout her formative years. She turned to eating to soothe her wounds. She used drugs to numb the pain. There were many times when she wanted to die.

The Brenda who reached out to me hated herself. She described it as a visceral, palpable self-loathing.

As I read Brenda's emotional outpouring, I unexpectedly felt the presence of my guides, Sanaya. They wanted me to pass a message along to Brenda. This had happened only once before when interacting with a stranger. I pulled out a tape recorder and entered an expanded state of consciousness to ensure I would capture their words verbatim.

The message to Brenda addressed challenges in her life that she had not revealed in her e-mail. The guides described years of digestive disorders caused by stuffing down her personal power and emotional pain. They detailed illnesses and life issues that only those with a bird's-eye view of Brenda's life could know.

Sanaya then provided Brenda with advice and specific tools to help her on her soul's journey. They gave her a mantra to repeat as she made what they declared would be permanent positive changes in her life.

The message from Spirit stunned both of us with its accuracy. All of it rang true to Brenda, and she took the guides' advice to heart, including the repetition of her new healing mantra. Those who knew Brenda may have wondered why she began to announce to all who would listen,

"I am free!" She and I recognized the words as a gift from Spirit that she would come to believe and embody.

The years of emotional stuffing eventually did catch up with Brenda in the precise areas of her body where Sanaya said she was prone to disease. On May 9, 2018, Brenda passed to the nonphysical world after a brief but heroic battle with bile duct cancer.

We had become dear friends by then. Our later correspondence and conversations overflowed with joy, so different from where we started. After so many years of self-hatred, Brenda could not contain the love she had kept bottled up inside for so long.

Early in our friendship, I introduced Brenda to another beautiful soul named Lynette Setzkorn. The two women shared stunningly similar backgrounds. Like Brenda, Lynette was recovering from years of emotional and spiritual pain. She shared similar experiences of self-loathing arising from early religious teachings. Their meeting resulted in a friendship so immediate, so close, and so deep that those who knew them referred to them as "Brenette."

Brenda and Lynette followed me around the country, attending all my presentations and workshops. They laughingly dubbed themselves my "number one stalkers." I felt humbled to be their guide and to share my nonphysical guides' wisdom with such eager students.

What they learned from the teaching and from their own spiritual searching accelerated their emotional healing. Little by little, Brenda's "I am free" mantra became reality for both of them.

Lynette spent most of Brenda's last year at her house, caring for her dear friend. They talked endlessly about the afterlife and how all things connect. Lynette didn't hesitate during this time to let Brenda know that she was beautiful inside and out. Brenda allowed herself to truly hear the words, and she blossomed in spite of her sickness. She finally felt fully seen and welcomed the balm of her friend's love.

Brenda took her last breath with Lynette at her side. Later that evening, to my utter stupefaction, I felt Brenda's presence next to me as clearly as if she were there in physical form. I fully expected to connect with Brenda at some point after she passed but not after only six hours.

Her words came through as clearly as if she were speaking on the telephone.

Lynette's telling everyone, "She's gone," Brenda said in my mind, *And I'm like, "Gone where?" I'm right here, Suzanne!*

Stunned by the clarity of her communication, I grabbed my iPad and began typing the conversation verbatim. This was Brenda's unmistakable voice, complete with her delightfully sassy inflections. I could see her exaggerated facial expressions and humorous gestures in my mind's eye.

I looked up from my keyboard only long enough to say to Ty, "Don't talk to me! Brenda is here!"

Ty's eyes widened. He knew it had been just a few hours since we received the phone call announcing Brenda's passing.

Death had clearly not slowed Brenda down, for she pressed on with her message as I returned to my typing.

I'm here, Suzanne. I'm just right here. I see buildings and I see fields. I see whatever I want to see, so for now, I see all of you.

I knew that "all of you" referred to the kindred spirits in the private Facebook group that she and Lynette had started. They called themselves "Souls Awakening," and it was three core members of that group who had rallied around Brenda, flooding her with love and comfort in her final days.

I was keenly aware that anyone who hadn't personally experienced transdimensional conversations might doubt the authenticity of this unexpected exchange with a dead woman. I sent her a silent message: *I'm going to need some evidence, Brenda, so that others will know this is you.*

Seemingly undeterred by my request, Brenda pressed on. *We're gonna have a party tomorrow night, yes we are!*

I sensed that Brenda meant she wanted me to gather the members of "Souls Awakening" for an online get-together. She wanted to share with the group more details about her transition, with me serving as her spokesperson through a process known as channeling.

This is important stuff, she said, and then in a jarring non sequitur, she casually flicked her hand backward across her right shoulder in my mind's eye and saucily asked, *Like my boa?*

What? I typed in reply. Her question made no sense.

As I wrote the question, I was filled with the *knowing* that Brenda's cryptic mention of a boa held the proof that I had wordlessly asked for. Immediately after sensing this, she silently communicated to me that our dear friend Lynette would understand the reference.

I got it just for the party, she said.

After sharing more details about the ease of her transition, Brenda wrapped up this momentous visit with a final message that seemed to capture her lifetime in one short sentence: *It's all about Love, Suzanne. We got that part right.*

Brenda withdrew her presence, and I immediately showed the typewritten words to Ty. A retired Navy destroyer captain, he had every human reason to be skeptical of my claims that Brenda had just visited me from the spirit world. But Ty understood the importance I place on maintaining the highest ethics and honesty in spirit communication. Years of witnessing the jaw-dropping, "no other explanation" (or NOE) evidence from those across the veil had transformed him from skeptic to believer.

I shared with him my excitement at knowing that Lynette would be able to validate this unexpected visit based on Brenda's one simple question: *Like my boa?* I had no idea just how profound the underlying message contained in that cryptic question would turn out to be.

Because it was late and I didn't want to call Lynette, I sent the full transmission to her in an e-mail. I explained that I sensed there was a story connected with a boa that she would know about. If this was so, I asked her to share it with me as validation that our friend was far from dead and gone.

I awoke at 2:30. As my eyes adjusted to the darkness, I recalled Brenda's surprise visit. I peeked at Ty sleeping soundly beside me. I hesitated, afraid to disturb him, but I had to know if Lynette had read my e-mail. I picked up the phone lying on the bedside table and clicked through to my Gmail account. I squinted to read the unopened messages in my inbox without my reading glasses. Sure enough, there was a new e-mail from Lynette with the same subject line as my earlier message to her.

When I clicked on her response, I had no trouble reading the opening line. Three large letters stood out, telling me all I needed to know in one quick glance:

"O.M.G.!" Lynette had written, punctuating each letter with a period. "She used to ask me to tell her that story over and over. It's one that we discussed from our earliest conversations together."

In the three years I had known Brenda and Lynette, I had never heard any story with mention of a boa from either of them, and my skin erupted in goose bumps.

"Early on," Lynette wrote in her e-mail reply, *"we would talk about things like, you know, 'Are we really just people suits, housing a soul for a little bit?' And I was more on board with that concept than she was.*

"I told her about a story that I thought illustrated the concept very well that this life is more like a play and that our real lives take place once we're on the other side, flying around, like she is right now.

"Brenda loved the story. She loved it," Lynette emphasized. *"She even asked me to write the boa story down, because she was going to share it with you when you interviewed her on your radio show at the end of the month, but she got a little premature."*

I gave a wistful smile at Lynette's reference to our friend's passing. Brenda had agreed to join me live on the air and discuss details of the spiritual awakening that had allowed her to face her terminal diagnosis with courage and grace. We thought she would be able to last until the show aired. When she passed sooner than expected, I was saddened that she would be unable to share her wisdom with my listening audience.

Now, however, a far greater message began to reveal itself as Lynette provided the details of Brenda's favorite story.

"I told her of a summer my family spent in New York City," Lynette wrote. *"I was six or seven, utterly enchanted with the glamour of Zsa Zsa and Eva Gabor. They were princesses, so glittering and gorgeous and fabulous that they didn't even seem real to me, a small-town Oklahoma girl.*

"With my family, I was walking down Broadway late one night. We walked past a theater, and there was some sort of a play or movie or a variety show going on. Zsa Zsa was featured, only her glamour was gone. She was ordinary, plain, like

Cinderella after the ball, back to scrubbing floors for the wicked stepsisters. I was crushed. That wasn't my Zsa Zsa!

"We walked on by the theater and suddenly a side door flew open and out sailed Zsa Zsa. She was magnificent, in full Zsa Zsa regalia, with her blond hair, perfectly coiffed, her glittering gown, and a big, fat feather boa around her neck.

"She floated into a waiting limousine and was gone. It was a magical moment, and I suggested to Brenda that this is what our lives are like here*: We might be washer women, or hard-working field hands, or teachers, or social workers, but once we take that last breath and the curtain comes down on this play, we all sail out the back door just like Zsa Zsa, back to our full magnificence with a final exhalation."*

I raised my eyes from the phone's screen long enough to send a heartfelt thank you to Brenda for this miraculous message. She could have chosen any of thousands of details that I didn't know about her personal life to validate her unexpected visit from across the veil. Instead, she used a seemingly inconsequential question to convey a meaningful message for all humanity:

"Like my boa? We are actors on a stage. The bodies we inhabit are our costume, and one day when the curtain comes down, we will remove the costume—*unmask our higher selves—and return to our true magnificence."*

I resumed reading Lynette's e-mail and saw that she, too, recognized the brilliance in Brenda's choice of evidence: *"That's what she's showing us,"* Lynette wrote. *"She is like Zsa Zsa. She is fabulous, perfect, and whole . . . even more divine than she was in the play."*

The implications of this story are huge. Brenda's message from across the veil tells us there is no death and, ultimately, no separation. With Consciousness as the foundation of all life experiences, we are intimately connected to each other. We are indivisible from the one pulsating sea of pure potential and creativity from which all experience arises.

This verified visit by a discarnate soul one day after her passing shows us that this human reality is like a play, and the human body really is only a temporary costume masking who we really are.

"We are Magnificence personified" is Brenda's main lesson. Using the boa story to deliver this message is pure genius.

PREPARE FOR TRANSFORMATION

How would your life change if you knew that you and your story are but one aspect of your multidimensional nature? And what if you could use this awareness to choose your point of view at any time, resulting in greater guidance and insights, a heightened sense of connection with all that is, and perpetual peace?

You, the soul, came here to do exactly that. You came here for the experiences—good and bad—knowing you would be challenged. You also came here knowing you might become so caught up in the role of being human that you would lose awareness of your true nature as Consciousness in expression.

Welcome to Earth School. This is not an isolated, windowless classroom with pass-or-fail lessons. It's more like art school, where you get to dive in and get your hands dirty as you create something more beautiful than what has already been created.

The trouble is, when you forget you are a soul, Earth School can get a bit messy.

Brenda Baker cleaned up the mess before she left, allowing her to graduate with honors. In so doing, she was able to communicate immediately and help us recognize that all of us—no matter how wounded—have the chance to make the most of our time here.

The Awakened Way is the soul's answer to your earthly challenges. It is designed to show you how to shift from feeling dissatisfied and disconnected to being aware that you are part of an intelligent, creative, benevolent Universe and that you are lovingly guided every moment. As you maintain greater presence and follow this guidance, you make choices that are in alignment with your highest self and enjoy a purpose-filled existence.

Albert Einstein had it right in the 20th century when he stated that no problem can be solved from the same level of consciousness at which it was created. History continues to repeat itself because most humans are ignoring the higher levels where the solutions to our challenges lie.

It is time to embrace what I call 21st-century spirituality. This requires updating your belief system with the latest scientific discoveries about the nature of consciousness and the underlying reality. These findings, blended with ancient spiritual truths, bring you to a *knowing* that we are all connected at a level beyond this earthly realm.

Most self-help books focus on your human nature. They completely miss the point that you are both human and a soul. They fail to teach you to access the Source of solutions that is always available and will never steer you wrong.

This book is different. It is not a self-help book. It is a *Higher-Self* book that reorients your belief system and shows you how to approach your challenges from the soul's perspective, where the highest answers lie. It is a guide to living a consciously connected and divinely guided life.

Unlike most self-help books, this book acknowledges that at a deeper level, there is nothing wrong with you. If you disagree with this statement, you are simply so caught up in the role of being human that you have forgotten who you really are. This higher-level guide from higher guides is designed to reawaken you to *both* aspects of your wholeness: your human persona and the soul.

It is action oriented. Why? Because, in the wise words of Lynette Setzkorn, you can't think your way into right acting, but you can act your way into right thinking.

You may read information here that contradicts what you have believed your whole life. It may ask you to consider ways of looking at yourself and others that is different from what most humans have accepted since the birth of time.

Happily, more people are coming to understand that we exist eternally *beyond* time. As a species, we are evolving, and we understand that the world is no longer flat. It is multidimensional.

We are learning that life does not end with the death of the body—that Consciousness (with a capital *C*) is fundamental.

These truths form the foundation of this guidebook. It is critical to understand them if you are going to be a positive force in your family, in your workplace, and in a world that too often seems on the verge of chaos.

As human beings, we are students in Earth School. The problem is, the students are directing the curriculum and the content instead of our unseen helpers. The undergraduates are running the school, and many of them are completely misguided.

We have adopted beliefs and behaviors that are fundamentally false. We base our decisions on external input.

This is akin to insisting that the sun rotates around the Earth because that's how it appears from where you stand. The soul has the higher point of view, and it has much to teach you.

The change in perspective offered here will make the difference between feeling apart from those around you and knowing you are a part of one interconnected family of souls. As you turn up your inner Light, the entire world indeed grows brighter. For everyone's sake, it behooves each of us to not only do well in school but also, like Brenda, graduate at the top of the class.

To that end, this book contains two parts that you may read in any order as you feel guided. You are probably used to moving through chapters sequentially when you read. That is the linear path. This book is different. The contents are more like a buffet than a book. Browse or read through the entire buffet first, then return to choose what appeals to you most. This is the spiral path.

Parts of human life are linear. You celebrate birthdays one after another. Your soul's path, however, is circular. It evolves through every choice you make and every experience that results from those choices. You, the soul, came here to take on specific challenges based on your unique character traits. If you miss a learning opportunity in Earth School as your human path moves through linear time, the soul will pick it up in the next season or cycle. The trajectory is ever onward, ever upward, like a true spiral.

Your soul evolves most efficiently through what I call the three E's of living The Awakened Way®. These stand for *educate*, *experience*, and *engage*. To awaken to the soul's presence, you, the human expression of Consciousness, begin with the hope that there is something more than being only human. This hope propels you to:

- *Educate* yourself about metaphysics—life beyond the physical

- *Experience* the greater reality for yourself

- *Engage* with metaphysical beings and experiences yourself

Through this ongoing cyclical process, you move from hope to belief. Over time, as you continue educating yourself, having greater and more wondrous inner and outer experiences and engaging fully with unseen teachers and your loved ones across the veil, you arrive at the ultimate reward: the remembrance and full *knowing* of who you really are and why you are here.

Part I consists of foundational information to assist you in the "educate" aspect of the three E's. These are the basics that your inner teacher—the soul—wishes to bring to your conscious awareness. At the soul level, you already know these things. For this reason, some of the teachings will resonate deeply. Others may create a sense of dissonance, thanks to the ego.

Ego is the aspect of your human self that supports the story. If you had no story, you would have no ego. You need ego to operate in your role as an individual. Its task is to differentiate your story from other people's stories. Ego isn't necessarily a bad thing, but issues can get a bit one-sided when ego does its job too well. If you sense defensiveness or fear as you read information here that is new to you, that's ego protecting itself.

To counter any resistance, I have interspersed the teaching with evidence-filled stories like Brenda's first visit from across the veil. These NOE experiences validate the existence of the greater reality of which you are a part. It has been scientifically proven that hearing stories of others' experiences not only expands your own beliefs but also opens you to having similar experiences.

Regardless of your current beliefs, test everything in your heart moment by moment. You may discover that as you acquire new information, practices, and experiences, your belief system evolves. Pick up this book a year from now, and parts that you may have had difficulty understanding or believing in the past will now resonate. The words will not have changed; you will have.

Part II is the "how to" part of this manual. It contains the tools your soul wants to share so you can experience, engage, and get reacquainted. Here you will learn step-by-step practices for expanding your state of awareness and directly communicating with nonphysical teachers, guides, and loved ones who have passed. You will learn how to receive answers to your greatest questions and gain insights into your deepest challenges. You will be guided how to validate that these interactive connections are not your imagination.

You will discover simple exercises that help you instantly refresh and recharge at the physical, mental, and emotional levels. You will learn techniques for healing yourself and your relationships on both sides of the veil. You will, by the end of this book, know how to find and maintain a state of peace, no matter what is going on around you.

You may have come to this material as the result of an unexpected life challenge or after years of spiritual seeking. Seek no more. The results you can look forward to are not promises for some far-off day. Adjust your belief system, do the practices, and you will notice yourself making new and healthier choices immediately.

I'm grateful to embark on this journey together. I'm excited for you. Trust me: you are fully capable of coming to know peace from within firsthand and feeling the joy that arises spontaneously as soon as you begin aligning with your true nature.

You came here in physical form to live fully. Your purpose as a soul is to experience LIFE. This is an acronym you will see repeatedly in the pages ahead, so it's good to memorize it now. It stands for *love in full expression*.

Perhaps until now, you have believed that heaven is some far-off place that can only be experienced when you die. That *BS* is far from the truth.

Heaven is a state of consciousness, a state of mind. You will soon discover and experience for yourself that there is only One Mind and One World from which all minds and worlds arise.

What do you do, then, when this human world gets you down? *The Awakened Way* makes the answer quite clear: you realize this is not the only world.

And this Awareness, dear soul, makes all the difference in the world.

PART I

THE FOUNDATIONS

PREFACE TO PART I

———

Are you familiar with the phrase "to grok"? It comes from the 1961 novel *Stranger in a Strange Land* by Robert Heinlein. The main character is a human raised on Mars whose English language is peppered with Martian words. "To grok something" means to wrap your head around a concept.

Until you grok your true nature, you may feel like a stranger in a strange land. That's because you are! You are a soul temporarily playing the role of a human being in a physical body on planet Earth.

You are in this world but not of it.

Until you truly, deeply understand this, you will experience a lingering feeling of homesickness without understanding why. You will suffer from an underlying sense that something is missing and do many silly things to fill that invisible hole.

Trust me: at the level of the soul, you lack nothing. You are immensely cared for at all levels of your being, for you are a direct expression of Divine Love. All that is missing at the human level is the awareness that what you are seeking to fill from the outside world is already present within you.

Your true Home is not a physical place but a state of being that you will learn more about in this section. Please don't read the following pages as you would a novel. Even though they are filled with true stories with stunning evidence to back up the truths they share, you will want to read slowly and carefully. Pause to reflect whenever something catches your attention.

The information here is deep. It is not dinnertime conversation material. Most everything ahead challenges the standard human concepts of reality, yet every word offers you the most divine release from the misery of thinking this is all there is or that you must go through life alone.

This is the only book you will ever need to end the homesickness.

Grok the content that follows and you will have found your way Home and rediscovered you are so very loved.

THE SOUL
KNOWS

———

Is there a part of you that has access to information you haven't yet learned or experienced? Yes. Awareness is not limited to your human mind. There is much more to you than meets the eye. Literally.

A young man named Wolf made a rough pencil sketch of an eye in one of his last acts before being killed by what some might call an act of nature. His drawing comes to mind often when I think about the nature of the soul. Wolf knew the profound symbolism of the eye as the bridge between the light you can see and the light that burns within you.

I met Wolf's parents at a conference in Virginia Beach, where I was one of the speakers. Mike and Beth Pasakarnis came in search of answers about their son's death and information about the afterlife. I recall the moment I showed a photo of Susan as part of my PowerPoint presentation. When I shared that Susan had been killed by a lightning strike, Beth's arm shot out and latched on to Mike's knee.

At the conclusion of my talk, Mike approached me. I noticed the large wolf's face on his T-shirt, but what grabbed my attention more was the intensity of his gaze. "My son was killed by a lightning strike," he said, looking directly into my eyes, "just like your stepdaughter."

I had no idea that I was about to embark on a journey of discovery with Mike and Beth that would culminate in sacred spiritual teachings and a powerful message for all humanity.[1]

Mike's immediate question was how his son could have known the exact manner and location of his impending death. Without yet hearing the details of Wolf's passing, I replied, "The soul knows more than our human side is aware of."

The story Mike then shared with me validated the truth of this statement.

Wolf lived alone in Plymouth, Massachusetts. He was chatting with friends at a favorite hangout when he suddenly rose and announced, "I have to go now." On his way home, he stopped to leave a heart-shaped stone as a gift for the owner of a local shop. That was the last time anyone saw him alive.

Police found his body on the ground next to a large birch tree in the historic Burial Hill cemetery. At first they suspected that the young man might have tried to climb the tree and had fallen to his death. Upon hearing the devastating news, Mike and Beth disagreed with the detectives' theory. At 29 years of age, Wolf had no reason to climb trees. They reported that the old tree was a favorite spot where Wolf sat to meditate, sketch, and compose poetry.

---

1   I tell the full story in my book *Wolf's Message* and in my YouTube video "Heart Gifts." This is the same presentation discussed in the Introduction to this book that transformed Brenda Baker's life.

Although prohibited from seeing their son's body until officials had ruled out foul play, Mike and Beth drove to Plymouth to feel closer to him. At a loss for what to do or how to process their grief, they stopped on the way at a local florist and bought two red roses as a tribute for Wolf. Each flower came with a green plastic sleeve that would allow them to place the stems upright in the ground.

Upon arriving at the cemetery, they easily found the tree, identified by Wolf's favorite hat lying on the ground close to the trunk. Mike and Beth gazed around at the litter left behind by the paramedics. They were distraught at the thought that their son might have suffered. With no answers and heavy hearts, they placed the two long-stemmed roses side by side at the base of the tree.

The next day, the coroner announced that a lightning strike was the cause of Wolf's death. Only then did one of the detectives assigned to the case recall the highly localized storm that had passed through town around the time of Wolf's passing. Locals claimed they heard just a single crack of thunder that afternoon.

With foul play ruled out, the police gave Mike and Beth Wolf's belongings and permission to enter his apartment. Mike had been there to visit only two days earlier. Had he known his son would be gone the next day, he never would have left.

Upon entering Wolf's home, the first thing the couple noticed was how uncharacteristically neat everything was, as if Wolf were expecting guests. To strangers, the place might seem anything but orderly. Wolf's black-and-white sketches, handwritten poems, and posters adorned every bit of wall space throughout the apartment.

Wolf usually changed the art arrangement every few months, but he had recently told his father, "I'm done moving things around, Dad."

Not even the furniture escaped Wolf's paintbrush. Mike often said that his deceased mother would have been mortified at the sight of her white sofa covered with unusual figures, shapes, and hieroglyphic lettering with her grandson's bright acrylic paints.

Emotionally drained, Mike sank onto the hand-me-down couch while Beth wandered through the remaining rooms.

"Mike, you have to see this!" she called out from the back.

He followed Beth's voice to what Wolf referred to as the Nature Room. Unlike the mix-and-match personal artwork in the rest of the apartment, this room usually displayed only full-color posters and photos of flora and fauna.

Stepping into the room, Mike's gaze fell immediately upon a piece of paper tacked to the wall. He knew it had not hung there during his visit two days prior. As was his custom, he had wandered throughout the entire apartment at that time, looking to see what was new.

The paper now stood out for its newness and because it was the only black-and-white hand-drawn piece in the room. A wooden chair had been centrally placed in front of the wall, as if inviting guests to sit and ponder this unique work of art.

A poem written in Wolf's slanted handwriting filled most of the 8½-by-11-inch page. The stanzas wrapped around a pencil sketch of a human eye. In place of a solid-colored cornea, Wolf had drawn a yin-yang symbol in the center, with hash marks outlining the contours of the eyelids.

Still reeling at the news that his son had been struck dead by a random act of nature, Mike forced himself to focus as he digested what were clearly his son's final written words.

"Spirit of Great Healer," the poem began, "awaken from within this Heart. Peace and tranquility flow like water."

Mike continued to the last line. His eyes widened in disbelief as he read, "The time has come to allow the light of nature to free my soul."

It is these words that Mike pointed out to me in his quest for understanding. He couldn't understand how his son could foresee that a bolt of lightning or what Wolf referred to as "the light of nature" would take the spirit from his body.

Mike further shared with me that Wolf's favorite T-shirt featured a white lightning bolt down the front. Equally incomprehensible was why Wolf had neatly cut out the square of fabric with the lightning bolt graphic and tacked it to the wall in the Nature Room directly opposite his prophetic poem.

Actions such as these are impossible to comprehend without an awareness of a greater reality beyond this earthly realm. I was grateful to be able to talk about the soul with Mike, because this understanding helped to explain yet more astounding details that surfaced three weeks after Wolf's death . . .

Once again it was Beth who discovered more stunning evidence that Wolf had foreseen events surrounding his death. She followed a nudge to reread his final poem and noticed something in the sketch of the eye that she had missed before. Incredulous, she called out, "Mike! I don't believe this!"

He looked at what she was pointing out and his breath caught in his throat. Wolf had included more than just a series of random hatch marks on the right side of the hand-sketched eye. He had drawn the distinct shape of the gnarly old beech tree where his lifeless body was found. And there, at the base of its thick trunk stood two roses, exactly as Mike and Beth had placed them.

I questioned Mike about their decision to place the roses by the tree. He assured me that his family had no tradition of honoring the deceased with flowers. They had never performed any kind of devotional ceremony with roses prior to Wolf's passing.

Clearly, Wolf had known the precise place and manner of his death, and he accurately drew a scene depicting what would happen in the aftermath of his passing.

Most people, when they hear this story, are astounded by Wolf's efforts to let us know that the human part of us is just the tip of a metaphorical iceberg. One man, however, became quite angry. He felt that if Wolf so clearly knew how, when, and where he was going to pass, he should have tried to change the outcome.

This is the way humans reason when they fail to see the bigger picture. It is human nature to become angry and judgmental when others' acts don't measure up to what we consider right and just. A shift in focus to the soul's perspective changes how we think and feel about events at this level.

Yes, his family suffered when Wolf passed. They miss his physical presence every day. I know this because Ty and I have become dear friends with Mike and Beth. But we can see that tens of thousands of people have learned and grown spiritually because of Wolf's transition. Their lives have been changed for the better by hearing Wolf's story, coming to know they are more than only human.

Thanks to Wolf, we know beyond a doubt that the soul has the bigger picture. The soul does not view death the way most humans do. To the soul, death is as natural as birth. It is the start of a new chapter in the ongoing flow of the soul's experiences.

This higher perspective brings peace and understanding to the process of dying and also to living. The soul knows that grief is a natural component of the human experience.

Wolf, just like your loved ones who have passed, is far from dead and gone. He proved this quite clearly in an unexpected way after I arranged to do a reading for Mike and Beth. Two days before our scheduled session, I awakened in my darkened bedroom to the awareness of a presence. Only when the image of Mike and Beth flashed onto the screen of my mind did I realize this was their son who had stopped by early for a visit.

Mindful not to awaken Ty, I reached for the pen and paper that I keep on the nightstand for just such an occurrence. Wolf clearly knew I needed evidence to validate this unexpected drop-in from across the veil, and he filled my mind with things I could not have guessed about his life. I later tallied 45 unique pieces of information that he shared with me in that brief initial visit.

He parted with the request that I "have Mike and Beth score this, like Gary."

"Gary" referred to Gary E. Schwartz, Ph.D., a professor at the University of Arizona. The renowned afterlife researcher has tested my ability in communicating with discarnate beings on multiple occasions as part of his work as director of the university's Laboratory for Advances in Consciousness and Health.[2]

Dr. Schwartz utilizes a formalized system to validate the evidence that comes through in a session with a medium. Families of those in spirit give a numerical score to each piece of information provided by the medium and must provide a written justification for their individual ratings.

---

2   See https://lach.arizona.edu

I obeyed Wolf's wishes and asked Mike and Beth to score the veracity of each of the items Wolf told me about himself. These were not generic traits and activities that one would expect from a young American male. Instead, Wolf's parents validated such unusual details as his interest in druids, his penchant for wearing robes, and his expressed desire for peace for all humanity despite my sense that he was a bit of a loner.

The accuracy of the information and the fact that I had no feedback during this encounter prompted Dr. Schwartz to declare it a "historic" visit from across the veil.

I asked Mike and Beth not to provide any feedback until after we had our reading by phone. That session gave me even more insights into Wolf's life as well as details about his passing that I could not have known. The evidence revealed in both conversations with Wolf's soul removed any doubt that consciousness continues beyond the transition we call death.

Wolf ended our profoundly evidential session with the promise, "I'll be around."

True to his word, he made his presence known multiple times in the following months with stunning clarity. He is one of the most powerful beings I have connected with in my years of communicating with Higher Consciousness. Each time he visited, he left me stuttering and awed by the high vibration of his energy and the depths of his love.

THE AWAKENED WAY

There have been people throughout history who have graced our planet to effect healing on a grand scale. They left a mark on humanity when we most needed their wisdom. Wolf is one such soul. The dramatic proof he left before his death that we are both soul and human compels us to pay attention.

Subsequent visits from Wolf in the months after I met his parents revealed the reason he went to such efforts to get our attention. He carried a message that is simple and timely: We as a species are out of balance. To find peace and tranquility and for our lives to flow like water, we need to spend less time in our logical, reasoning human mind and become reacquainted with the feeling–knowing part of ourselves: the soul.

As we do so, we will begin to enjoy the fruits of living an awakened life. By balancing the head with the heart—the human nature with soul awareness—we embrace who we really are and why we're here. We enjoy living what I call The Awakened Way. This is not a system, not a process, not a religion. It is a mindful approach to enjoying a consciously connected and divinely guided life.

With Wolf's guidance, I distilled his teachings into three truths that form the foundation of awakened living:

1. You are not only human.
2. You are part of one big web connecting all that is.
3. The creative and healing force of the Universe is Love.

Your normal waking consciousness is but one of limitless states that you can enjoy. Each state offers you unique experiences with its own "rule set." For example, in normal human awareness, you think of a goal, and you must take action to achieve it. This may take time and effort. In the dream state, there is no sense of time. Things seem to happen without your control. The same is true of expanded states of consciousness experienced through meditation.

We compare the dream state and meditative experiences to what we know as normal waking consciousness and refer to these as "altered" states. But what if the state of awareness you are experiencing now as you read these words and look around you is an altered state in relation to a less limiting form of Consciousness you're simply not aware of—that of the soul?

What we call "normal" refers to the embodied human experience. In the grand scheme of things, this is a temporary state. Countless people with near-death experiences and those who have altered their perception through meditation or psychedelic drugs have found themselves fully self-aware while gazing at their own body from outside of it. These people tell us that human awareness is stifling compared to the more expanded states they experienced when not limited by the "human in a body" rule set.

The expanded states of consciousness I achieved when I began meditating after my stepdaughter transitioned led me to experiences I didn't know were possible until I experienced them for myself. My initial goal was to discover if some part of Susan had survived her body's passing. As you know from reading the Introduction to this book, I accomplished that goal and much more.

With increased commitment to further adventures in consciousness, I encountered and engaged various non-physical beings who demonstrate creativity and intelligence far beyond my own. They are always helpful, healing, and nonthreatening, and I welcome these visits that provide insights into our true nature and a greater reality to which we all belong.

It was August of 2010 when I felt a noticeable shift in vibration during my daily practice. A powerful presence unexpectedly arose in my awareness. The energy felt both masculine and feminine. When I asked who this was, I heard the clear response, "We are a collective consciousness of your guides. You will write and write and write as 'Sanaya.'"

When I searched on the Internet for this name, I found various meanings. Some of the more meaningful descriptors include "eminent, distinguished, and of the gods" and "one worth knowing."

True to their promise, Sanaya has since given me thousands of daily messages, causing me to write and write and write for them. I further developed the ability to be their physical voice, sharing their messages aloud with audiences in venues that range from large ballrooms to intimate gatherings in my living room. To hear the words of Sanaya as they come through and to sit in the presence of their wise and loving energy is a palpable experience of Higher Consciousness.

Their messages speak to all of us as we face the challenges of being human. They remind us who we are at our core. In this way, they mirror the three principles of Wolf's message. Together, Wolf and Sanaya guide us to enjoy living lucidly as both human and soul.

Years after Sanaya first began working through me, a friend made a stunning discovery. She told me that she had randomly uncovered another meaning for my guides' name. It turns out that in addition to "one worth knowing," *Sanaya* also means "flash of lightning."

Susan, Wolf, and Sanaya share a connection to this powerful Force of Nature. It is the rare human who is not awed by lightning. At a subconscious level, perhaps we recognize that the same power that flows through a bolt of lightning flows through us, albeit at vastly reduced voltage.

This Force, this Light, is indivisible, leaving everything connected at the deepest level. And what do we call such complete and absolute connection?

We call it Love.

It's a good thing that the brain acts as a filter for this powerful energy that is all around us. If the full force of the Love that is our essence were allowed to flow through us unimpeded, our bodies could not handle it.

Still, some of that loving energy does manage to pass through the filter when it serves the greater good. Two days before my stepdaughter Susan was struck and killed by lightning, she came to me quite clearly in a dream. It was so vivid that I described it to Ty upon awakening. Susan and I were at a party. She walked up to me, looked directly into my eyes, and assured me, "The baby and I are fine."

I have since learned that dreams such as this that are intensely clear and convey an important, positive message are actual visits from the soul. No one in our family, including Susan, had any indication at the human level that she and Liam would be leaving us so soon. Her soul, however, knew that I would receive and deliver this reassuring message.

Skeptics might dismiss my interpretation of this predictive dream. I understand the natural tendency for humans to distrust that which we can't prove with our physical senses. Therefore, I'm grateful to a young man nicknamed Wolf, who left such stunning and irrefutable proof that the soul knows when its time on earth is ending.

The stories I have shared so far in this book are anecdotal yet filled with verified evidence that this physical reality is not the only existence. Brenda, Wolf, Susan, and

Sanaya serve as messengers who speak directly to the soul. This eternal part of you is eager to integrate its presence into your daily life so that you can flow through your days with greater ease.

The pages that follow contain information that may seem new to you at the human level. At the level of the soul, it is simply a review.

YOU ARE THIS

———

There's a song that comes on our Pandora station in which Christina Perri laments, "but I'm only human!" Every time I hear her sing this, I stop what I'm doing and echo a reply, stretching out the third word to two syllables, "No, you're not!"

If my husband is around, we laugh in unison. Ty is the first to admit he is not in the same place spiritually as I am, but we've been together on this journey of awakening long enough that he recognizes the truth in my response: we are far more than these bodies.

What we need is a powerful hit song with lyrics that help people around the world realize that we are both human and a soul, and something so much greater rolled into one glorious whole.

Words are powerful. They shape our reality far more than you may realize. Take "God" as a very relevant example. What comes to mind when you read or hear the name "God"? Pause for a moment and reflect on the meaning you give to your concept of a supreme deity and how this makes you react.

Does the name "God" cause you to feel open and uplifted, or do you have a bit of "history" with God that causes your stomach to clench?

Notice that we are discussing *your* concept of a supreme deity. This indicates that others' concepts may differ. If there is—as most cultures agree—only one God, then how can they differ at all?

They differ because most of us acquire our understanding of God from other people. You likely gained your perceptions from family members, teachers, priests, preachers, rabbis, gurus, friends, books, and other sources, including, yes, even song lyrics. In other words, most people base their definition of the most powerful force in existence on what others have told them.

This is akin to being told the sun rises above the horizon, and you accept this as truth without investigating for yourself what's really going on. Blind acceptance about the nature of God has led to misconceptions and conflicts that span families, communities, and cultures.

I remember discussing one such conflict when invited to dine with some new friends in our neighborhood. For anonymity's sake I'll call them Rick and Sarah. As we enjoyed a meal in their lovely home, we asked the normal getting-to-know-you questions. When we got around to talking about their children, Sarah bemoaned the fact that their daughter, Becky, had embarked on a nontraditional career path.

Rick rolled his eyes and shook his head as Sarah described Becky's job that focused on mind, body, and spirit healing. It was clear that neither parent approved of their daughter's choice. I praised Becky for following her heart, but Sarah shook her head. Sarah then revealed that they were seriously concerned about Becky's mental health after she made "an outrageous claim" on social media.

Curious, I asked what it was that caused them such distress. Our hostess took a deep breath and said, "She publicly announced that she is God."

Aware of Rick and Sarah's discomfort, I held back a smile, but I totally understood why their daughter would make such a claim. The sound of a nearby clock became very loud as I pondered an appropriate response.

To my utter stupefaction, before I could share anything I had learned on my spiritual journey, my oh-so-left-brained husband replied, "Well . . . who's to say she's not?"

All three of us gaped at Ty, if not for different reasons. There was nothing in our new friends' belief system or experience to consider that their daughter was perfectly sane. As for me, I held my reaction until we got in the car, at which time I extended my arms and said, "Honey! You really DO get it!"

"Of course, I do!" he exclaimed, looking like a schoolboy who just earned a gold star. "I'm a New Age kinda guy!"

What Ty and I understand, and what we shared with Rick and Sarah, is that each of us serves as the physical arms, legs, and voice for the Guiding Organizing Designing (GOD) Source of all that is.[3] This intelligent Force that animates our body, mind, and spirit is not apart from us, but we are a part of it. Put another way: none of us is the entirety of God, but God is the entirety of us.

To claim that we are God sounds egotistical, if not blasphemous, for we are aware of our human limitations. Becky's claim might have been more easily digested if she had said, "I am God in expression."

I give Becky credit for speaking her truth. Most people are more concerned with what other people will think of

---

3   I credit Gary E. Schwartz, Ph.D., of the University of Arizona for this excellent acronym, featured in his 2006 book *The G.O.D. Experiments: How Science Is Discovering God in Everything, Including Us.*

them if they express nontraditional beliefs. We are taught not to question authority, and there are often consequences for those who do.

The soul isn't affected by such things. It's all-in for anything that might bring more harmony into its experiences. Couple the soul's innate courage with some open-minded curiosity, and you will be looking at real personal transformation.

QUESTIONING WHAT YOU BELIEVE

In my work, I encounter many who left their childhood religion because some of its tenets no longer sit well with them. They question what they were told and are no longer able to visualize God in the image of a judgmental being who doles out favors with conditions. They are guided by new heart-based beliefs and an inner sense of knowing truth.

So, why don't we ask a few questions designed to help you understand the nature of Divinity and your connection with it? We'll begin with one that gets right to the heart of the issue: *What is the same in every human being and doesn't change as you age?*

We'll work our way to the answer with a brief exercise. Please reply in full sentences, beginning each response with the words "I am," as shown in the parentheses:

- How old are you?
  ("I am _____ years old.")

- What is your gender?
  ("I am a _____.")

- What roles do you play in your family?
  ("I am a _____ and a _____" etc.)

- What is your occupation?
  ("I am a _____.")
- What is your nationality?
  ("I am a(n) _____.")
- What is your personality like?
  ("I am _____.")
- What is your political leaning?
  ("I am _____.")
- How tall are you?
  ("I am _____ feet _____ inches tall.")

Perhaps you can think of some more descriptors along these lines, but by now you have the idea.

All the answers you provided above are elements of "The Story of You." They comprise your prime human identity, along with your name, your memories, accomplishments, successes, and failures. In short, your story contains everything an author would include if they were writing your biography.

So, let's imagine that you wake up one morning with a case of complete amnesia. Your mind is a blank slate. You can't remember a single detail about yourself. Everything you've ever learned about the world has been wiped clean from your memory bank. Words hold no meaning. You look at your hand and don't know what it is. You look in a mirror and don't know who or even what you're seeing.

In other words, you find yourself in the same situation as a newborn baby.

What is the one thing that you would know, even without words?

Just as you knew it in the moment you were born and the moments that followed, *you would know that you exist.*

The words we use to express this concept are "I am."

"I" is the pronoun we use to reference the self. "Am" is the verb that references a state of being. "I am" indicates self-awareness of being.

In the space between all words, all thoughts, all memories, what do you know with certainty?

"I exist and I am aware of it."

When stating, "I am," all self-aware beings are referring to an identical experience. Each person's sense of self-awareness is colored by unique experiences that follow their first breath and accumulate over a lifetime. It is these contents of the stories that differ. But no matter one's age or life history, "I am"—the awareness of *being*—is a *shared* phenomenon.

With this in mind, let's return to our original question: What is exactly the same in every human being and doesn't change as you age?

The answer is: the part of you beyond your story.

Think of "I am" like the vast, open sky. Any words that follow "I am" are clouds. They arise within the sky, temporarily changing the appearance of it, but they have no effect on the sky's basic existence.

Who are you beyond your story? You are the open sky, my friend—the presence and expression of an immense Awareness that knows it exists. Because this is a shared presence, it's more fitting to refer to this as the Absolute Self (with a capital *S*) as opposed to the temporary, limited sense of "my"self with a story.

Since we're capitalizing words, let's do so with the "being" form of the verb, "AM." Have you seen "I AM" written this way? This is how it's usually written in the Bible, in the Book of Exodus. The story goes that when

Moses asked for God's name, the first response he received was, "I AM that I AM."

So, we have the Absolute "I AM" that is everywhere, all-knowing, and all-powerful. And we have over seven billion relative beings also claiming "I am." The difference between relative awareness and Absolute Awareness is the individual stories or experiences that arise in the one I AM Awareness, like clouds in the sky. The Self is the sky. The selves are the clouds.

You are not apart from the sky. You are intimately part of it as a self-aware expression of self-awareness. You cannot separate Awareness. What this means is that your fundamental nature is complete, whole, and indivisible.

What keeps unawakened human beings from realizing they are a direct expression of this infinite Source? They identify with the elements of a temporary story and overlook that which is always present, whole, and never changes.

Your story is real. It arises from the one Self. But when you as the temporary expression of the Self take your self-awareness so seriously that you believe you are alone and separate, you suffer.

We call this seemingly separate self the ego. Just like The Story of You, the ego is very real, and it is a natural outcome of the human experience. What is not real is the sense of separation that ego often creates. The idea that we could ever be separate from our true essence is an illusion. Just as you can't separate the clouds from the sky, you can't separate the self from the Self.

So, is the Self God?

Rather than trying to agree upon a name for what is beyond our ability to name, I prefer to focus on the attributes of The Ultimate that we can identify. These would include:

- Omniscience
- Omnipotence
- Omnipresence
- Self-awareness
- Limitless intelligence
- Indivisibility
- Being-ness

In trying to define the nature of Divinity, I tell the story of a woman who asked Thomas Edison for the definition of electricity. He looked her squarely in the eyes and replied, "Madame, electricity *is*. Use it."

This self-aware state of Being with all the attributes above simply *is*. Depending on whether your approach is philosophical, spiritual, religious, or scientific, you may give this being-ness different labels: Source, Force, the Unified Field, Universal Awareness, Pure Consciousness, God, the Light, Presence, Infinite Intelligence, and so forth.

Perhaps this is why some religions forbid its adherents to state God's name aloud. To do so is to put a limitation on that which has no limits.

Personally, I gravitate toward "Wholeness," which to me has the same connotation as total connection. As I stated previously, *love* is the word we use when we experience a connection with something or someone. Therefore, *love* is "lack of separation." With this definition, you can understand now why we say, "God is Love."

I remember exactly where I was when I had the visceral experience of being connected with all that is. I wasn't standing on some mountaintop. I had just finished brushing my teeth and had turned to leave the bathroom when a song with powerfully uplifting chords came from speakers in the bedroom. A feeling of what can only be described as Divine Love welled up within me and over-flowed. I raised my arms to the sky and twirled in place. This feeling of indescribable bliss had no discernible cause. I had heard the same song before without this powerful surge of unbridled joy.

Was this experience of total connection bestowed upon me because I had achieved perfection? Not at all. My life at the time—as it is for all of us in every moment—was a mixture of white puffy clouds, some gray ones scattered here and there, and a big black thunderhead looming on the horizon in the form of my elderly mother's declining health. Yet, for an instant, a gust of clarity allowed me to see beyond the current conditions and know that all was well, *no matter what.*

In that moment of grace, the realization hit me that the Guiding, Organizing, Designing Force I had been looking for outside of me was right here, looking through my eyes. It was the sky and the clouds. I was the sky and the clouds. There was no separation.

You mean, this *is what everyone is searching for?* I thought as the enormity of this realization hit me.

The discovery had two sides. I felt downright giddy knowing that the secret was out and the search was over. At the same time, I experienced a frightening letdown that this Aware Presence I had dedicated so much time and effort seeking was so immensely ordinary that I had overlooked it.

The disparity between our concept of an all-powerful being and our experience of our humanity was all too apparent. How could Divinity be experiencing life through me? It was quite apparent that neither I nor anyone I know is all-knowing and all-powerful.

And then I reminded myself of the many miracles that had led me to this realization—those moments when the clouds parted and there was no other explanation (NOE) than that we are part of something so much greater than our stories. (Rest assured, I will share more of these NOE moments with you in the coming pages.)

Yes, I realized, this sense of simply "being" is ordinary and easily overlooked. What is *extraordinary* is the fact that "this" somehow knows every hair on my head and those of over seven billion of my fellow human beings.

"This" is undivided wholeness. Thousands of people who have had near-death experiences (NDEs) describe the same sense of knowing that all is connected, just as I experienced in my spiritually transformative event (STE). They speak of being swept up in a dynamic, flowing river of light or being approached and even "embraced" by a loving presence unlike anything they ever encountered in physical form.

All that arises in awareness, including you, is an expression of this infinite Light.

"This" is your true nature. "This" is you, beyond your story. As long as you, the Presence of Awareness, are playing a role in The Story of You, Awareness appears limited. "This"—limited or not—remains ultimate, Absolute Awareness. The rest is relative.

"This" is the space in between your thoughts, and it is the source of your thoughts. It is ever-present, timeless, and formless. It is self-aware. It is whole, complete, and indivisible. This part of you is the same in me and everyone you have ever and will ever meet.

"This" is the meeting place that kindred spirits refer to when they greet each other with the Sanskrit salutation and say, "Namaste." Said with meaning, the heart opens to the mutual message in this one, simple word: "I honor the place in you that is of love, of light, of truth, and of peace. When you are in that place in you and I am in that place in me, we are one."

Recognition of this place that takes up no space and all space takes us Home, right here, right now, for there is only Here, when you come to know "This," which is as close as your breath.

In the beginning was Oneness. Then You, Awareness, went off on a little journey to experience otherness—something other than simply being. You are both Absolute Awareness and its relative experiences. You and I and everyone else is a point of view of the Oneness.

The story is not the entirety of Awareness, but Awareness is the entirety of the story. The aspect of You that you identify with moment by moment—your innate wholeness or the limited story—determines your peace.

Are you ready to reclaim your fundamental wholeness? Call it Source, call it the Life Force, call it Consciousness, Awareness, Father, Mother, or God, or celebrate as I do and call it Joy!

Call it what you like, but *use it*:

- To recognize you have always been whole

- To understand why you cannot ever be alone

- To experience a sense of completeness no matter what is going on in the story

- To know you are so very loved

To be separate from "This" is impossible. You are This. Here. Now. Aware Awareness *Being*.

STUFF HAPPENS

How can you be both human and a soul at the same time?
Both are simply aspects of one state of being. Look at the word
love as an analogy. You can write it in block letters or cursive
writing. In the former, you see each letter as stand-alone and
separate. In the latter, the letters are connected, with one
flowing into the other. You are like that. You can see each
person as stand-alone and separate or change the way
you view each other and realize nothing is really separate
but one flow of information-energy that is all connected.
You are so very loved.

— Sanaya

I was pondering the best way to describe what reality is made of when I had a visit from the deceased daughter of my friend Irene. Carly passed at age 24 from esophageal cancer. I never met her in physical form, but I have come to know her quite well since I gave Irene a reading in 2014.

These days, Carly usually drops in on me while I am thinking about her mother. This is not surprising, as we are all connected at the energetic level. If two or more people have a history of interacting, the result is analogous to the scientific phenomenon known as quantum entanglement.

When you entertain thoughts of those with whom you're entangled—whether in a body or not—your thoughts excite the shared energetic field that your interactions over time have created. If the person you're thinking about is sensitive, they will pick up on your energetic signature and think of you in return.

That's what happened with Carly. She sensed me thinking about her mother. I knew that Irene had gone with her husband, Tony, to see the movie *Top Gun: Maverick*. I was wondering how they liked it when Carly dropped in. Without any greeting, Carly filled my mind with an image of Irene sitting in the theater holding her hands in front of her face as if she couldn't bear to watch what was on the screen.

I silently asked Carly, *Why would your mom avert her eyes?*

Carly seemed pleased with herself as she sent me a silent, *You'll see.*

I smiled in awareness at this little game we played. Irene's specific behavior didn't matter to Carly. She simply wanted her mom to know that she had been with her in the theater.

Less than an hour later, Ty and I walked around the corner to Irene and Tony's house to enjoy dinner together. Within a minute of greeting each other, Irene exclaimed, "Oh, that movie! I loved it, but I was like this at the end!" She cupped her hands in front of her face.

"Oh! You beat me to it!" I exclaimed. "Carly dropped in on me earlier today and showed you to me in that exact pose."

"The final scene when Maverick and Rooster almost got shot down," Irene explained, "I couldn't stand it!"

We both clapped with excitement. Neither of us ever grew tired of these magical validations that our loved ones who have passed are still part of our lives. This awareness had transformed Irene from a bereaved parent to a powerful advocate for other parents with children across the veil. Today she serves tirelessly as vice president of the international support group Helping Parents Heal.

One of my favorite exchanges with Carly over the years occurred when she dropped in unexpectedly to announce with great indignation, *I'm NOT a prima donna!*

When I passed along this message, Irene burst into laughter. While leading a recent meeting of her local chapter of Helping Parents Heal, Tony reminisced about Carly. He shared that she had vowed to never wash a single load of laundry during her four years at Boston College. True to her word, every time she arrived home on a visit, she brought several Hefty bags of dirty clothes. He ended his story by stating, "Carly always was a bit of a prima donna."

As Carly so clearly showed, your loved ones who have passed hear your conversations and your thoughts. While they respect your privacy, they also see you and your surroundings more clearly than you might imagine. Carly proved this quite well one evening when Irene and I made a deliberate effort to connect with her. The two of us had escaped to the bonus room over Irene's garage while our husbands sat downstairs talking about fishing.

I connected quite easily with Carly, who is as chatty across the veil as she was in physical form. As always, Carly shared current events that Irene easily validated. Carly showed that she knew all about her stepsister's cold and a necklace that Irene had recently bought.

I was pleased with the clarity of our connection, but after a brief pause, I squinted in confusion. "I know this can't be right," I said, shaking my head. "Carly says there's a dog treat under the couch in your living room."

Irene laughed. Everyone who knew Irene teased her about her floor fetish. She mopped and vacuumed the entire house daily. We both agreed there was no way that even the smallest crumb of food could escape her mop, let alone a dog treat. And should such a transgression miraculously occur, our two low-slung dachshunds were running around the living room below us as we spoke. They would have hoovered up any food on the floor within minutes of our arrival.

Still, everything else Carly told us that evening was accurate, so we went downstairs to see for ourselves. Without saying a word to the men, Irene grabbed a flashlight and peered under the love seat. With a grim face, she stood up and gave me a disappointed shake of her head. No dog treat.

Puzzled, I made a face. I had learned to trust what those in spirit shared with me, and Carly had been quite clear.

"What are you looking for?" Tony asked.

"Carly says there's a dog treat under the couch," Irene replied.

"In your house?" Ty asked. "Unlikely."

"She said it's under the *couch*," I reported, emphasizing the last word. "That's a *love seat*."

All eyes moved to the longer sofa. A shiver of anticipation rippled through the room. I held my breath as Irene once again got down on her knees and shined the flashlight under the cushions.

"I don't believe it!" she squealed, as she stretched an arm under the couch. She pulled it back and extended her open hand, revealing a tiny brown rectangular dog treat.

Our two pups and Carly's goldendoodle, Linus, gathered around Irene with tails wagging. Their excitement paled in comparison with ours.

"I knew it!" I shouted as Irene and I high-fived.

She handed the dog treat to Tony for inspection, and both men shook their head.

"That," Ty said, "is over the top."

"How did Carly know it was there?" Tony asked.

I wondered the same thing, so I shifted my focus and asked her directly. What I heard left me chuckling. "She says she can see right through the furniture, like X-ray vision."

This was news to me, because until that day I hadn't given any thought to how those across the veil perceive our world. That exchange with Carly shifted my belief system yet again. In the days that followed, I asked my guides to share more with me about the different ways we experience reality.

I learned that the different dimensions are *relative* realities. We call the afterlife the "spirit" world, yet their world seems quite solid to them. We call ours the physical world, yet as Carly showed us, those in spirit see through our furniture and walk through walls. Solidity is relative.

Are there alternate ways of experiencing reality? Absolutely.

The allegory of *Plato's Cave* is ideal for understanding how our limited human viewpoint keeps us trapped. This age-old story shares the plight of a group of men imprisoned in a cave for the entirety of their lives. They are chained so that they face the back of the cave. When objects pass by a fire behind them, they see shapes and movement on the blank wall before them and give names to the shadows.

Their reality consists only of the cave, the wall, the shadows, and each other. They don't realize there is something beyond their current experience projecting the shadows onto the wall.

When those across the veil send us evidence of realities beyond our own, we make a choice to investigate further or dismiss these phenomena.

If you take the time to truly question reality, you will discover that everything that exists are experiences of the One Mind of Awareness seen through different viewpoints. What we call normal waking consciousness is only one viewpoint that Awareness can take. Other lenses through which you as Awareness experience reality while in human form are in dreams and expanded states achieved through meditation, bodywork, or psychedelic substances.

But why stop with the human point of view? There are other lenses through which to view reality. Don't allow fear of the unknown or of what other people will think to hold you prisoner.

As you come to know that you are "This"—pure Awareness *being*—you gain access to worlds upon worlds.

UNDERSTANDING AWARENESS

From the limited human point of view, the world appears to consist of individual solid parts. But you and the objective world are no more solid than the couch Carly could see through. Einstein proved that matter is energy. Another renowned scientist, David Bohm, described our reality accurately and quite poetically as "undivided wholeness in flowing motion."

You are Aware Awareness experiencing a continuous flow of sensations that give the *impression* of solidity, permanence, and individuality. But all is not as it seems.

Imagine the following scenario: You sit to meditate with the intention of experiencing yourself as the pure state of being. You willingly set aside your focus on your to-do list, your aches and pains, and the latest family drama. You take a deep breath and center your awareness on the heart. In doing so, your mind and body relax quite nicely, and you experience something akin to a vast ocean of stillness.

For about 30 seconds, you do a pretty good job of just "being." And suddenly, you become aware of a sensation. You are well familiar with this experience, and it is followed immediately by a thought that arises as if on its own to label the sensation "an itch."

And then you, the Presence of Awareness *being*, become aware of a follow-up thought that effortlessly bubbles up from the silence: *Should I scratch it?*

You allow the thought to pass by and return to "being." From the stillness you notice a stream of thoughts that arise despite your efforts to simply be the ocean: *I shouldn't scratch it. I'm supposed to be perfectly still.*

As these two thoughts subside, a feeling now arises in their wake. You don't need words to label the feeling. You know it well. Yet, a thought arises unbidden to label the feeling: *I am so* frustrated*!*

On and on it goes, this stream of interruptions. You could sit in a meditative state for eternity, and total stillness would remain elusive. The Sea of Consciousness will undulate, rising and falling with endless experiences, because that's what it does. The Sea is never still for long, and it is far from empty. It is filled with potential that simply must arise . . . as what? As waves of experience.

We call this activity of Awareness the Mind. When it becomes focused exclusively on one point of view, you call it "my mind," with a small *m*. This mind arises and subsides within the greater Mind. As you saw in the example above, the waves of experience can be categorized into three elements:

1. Sensations
2. Thoughts
3. Feelings

I use the acronym ST-F (pronounced "stuff") for these elements of experience.

Let's do a simple exercise so you can have the personal experience of ST-F arising.

Take a long, slow, relaxing breath to get centered (which means that your mind isn't jumping all over the place). When you feel relaxed, close your eyes and be still for about five to ten seconds. Do it now, please.

What were you aware of in those moments of silence? Give a name to one experience you had in those few seconds that were supposed to be still. Examples might include:

- I felt the air conditioning blowing on my neck. (sensation)

- I heard the clock ticking. (sensation)

- I wondered if I was doing it right. (thought)

- I felt peaceful. (feeling)

- I felt restless. (feeling)

- I felt _____.

How did you notice the sensation, thought, or feeling? Did you control it, or did it simply arise in awareness?

Let's do it again.

Just "be" Aware Awareness and notice what naturally arises . . .

What were you aware of? Was it a sensation, thought, or feeling?

So far, so good. Let's do it one more time. Close your eyes and be quiet, but this time don't experience any ST-F at all . . .

. . .

. . .

How did you do?

I apologize for asking you to do the impossible, but I did so for the important lesson that reveals itself: try as you might, *ST-F happens.*

You and the objective world only seem solid from your current human point of view. Ultimately, you are undivided wholeness in flowing motion. Experiences flow in an endless dance of sensations, thoughts, and feelings, whether you are in normal human waking consciousness, dreaming, or experiencing altered states of awareness. And the good news? You are not stuck in the limited and limiting experiences of The Story of You (state your name). All that exists is Mind and the experiences within it.

You, Aware Awareness, get to choose your point of view. You can choose to continue focusing on the experiences you can't predict or control, or you can go with the flow as the Experiencer. You can stay in the default point of view as a human being in a body, or you can shift your attention when you need a higher perspective and be the Observer of your story.

When Carly, Brenda, Susan, Wolf, or any others who are no longer in physical form drop in on me, they do so as experiences within the One Mind. My mind doesn't create them or invite them in. There is simply awareness of a *sensation* of lightheadedness, followed by the presence of *feelings* that identify unique and recognizable personalities that stand apart from my default point of view.

Thoughts such as *I'm not a prima donna!* arise in awareness and are noticed because they are so clearly not part of my personal story. Great joy results as this flow of experiences is shared with those who are not yet trained to notice the more subtle ST-F.

Wolf Pasakarnis was well aware of the greater web that connects us all. He told me quite clearly that when he walked in a body he felt as if he were living in two worlds at once. His artwork reflects how challenging this proved to be for him. One rather dark drawing is reminiscent of the prisoners in *Plato's Cave*. In it, Wolf drew a bright-red heart crisscrossed with heavy, metal links. Next to the heart he wrote the words, "I long to be free of the chains that hold my heart captive."

With awareness and intention, you can drop the shackles, turn around, and step out of the cave of self-imposed isolation. As you turn up the light of Awareness, the shadows disappear. You discover that emptiness is actually fullness, and separation is an illusion.

ALL IS NOT
AS IT SEEMS

———

At the surface you may feel at times separate and alone, but within you is a knowing that you are part of a whole. And you are, dear soul. The human part of you may not see this now, but part of the soul's task is to peck away at your human shell until the Light that joins all that is peeks through. And once it does, oh, my, you will have found that all souls are your "peeps."
You are so very loved.

— Sanaya

You now understand that all experiences—all sensations, thoughts, and feelings—whether you call them "mine" or "yours"—arise from one shared I AM *being*. From this most basic, unmodified sea of pure potential, anything can arise.

I hope you find this exciting! In Part II of this book, you will learn to shift your attention at will to tune in to other channels of reality. When you are willing to set aside your "only human" belief system, you open yourself to a world of adventures in consciousness.

I experienced one such adventure on Christmas Day during my morning meditation. That holiday morning, I asked for the gift of an encounter with any higher being who could help me travel to their world. Almost immediately, I became aware of a very powerful masculine presence.

I usually feel rather than see those who come to visit. In this case, I not only sensed this man's immense strength and wisdom but also saw his features quite clearly. He appeared as an old man with an impressive beard and long white hair, much like pictures I had seen of Moses.

Who are you? I asked from my mind to his.

The reply came in a single word: *Odin.*

I scanned my memory. I had heard the name Odin, but I had no recollection of who he was.

What can you tell me about you? I asked silently.

In response, he showed me a flying horse, and I smiled. Such an image pushed the boundaries of my belief system, but I had learned to play along with whatever unfolded.

Suddenly, I experienced a piercing pain. It was sharp enough that I yelped and doubled over as my hands slid to the left side of my torso. Those in spirit often give me tangible symptoms in my body as evidence of injuries they suffered or how they passed. I made a mental note of the pain, and it immediately subsided.

Odin comes to teach you the secret of the runes, he said. He added, *There is much wisdom there.*

Hearing the word *runes* startled me. I knew about this divination tool thanks to Wolf, who included runic symbols in much of his artwork.

A stream of insights followed, and I wrote them on the pad of paper I kept on my lap during meditation for just this reason.

Runes allow you access to the subconscious, Odin said. *They are merely patterns. See the one shaped like a lightning bolt. It holds great meaning for you.*

Is there one shaped like a lightning bolt? I asked.

What do you think? he replied.

I felt both chastised and excited at the same time. I felt certain from this response that I would find a lightning bolt among the runes' 24 symbols.

When his powerful presence withdrew, I came out of meditation and headed directly for my laptop. Upon Googling "Odin," I experienced full-body goose bumps. According to Northern European mythology, I learned, Odin is the All-father of the Norse gods. He has long been revered as the mouthpiece of god who communicates spiritual knowledge and wisdom.

I had asked to speak to a master, and Infinite Intelligence sent a good one!

Online images of Odin depicted a man with long white hair and a beard, exactly as he had appeared to me. Several of the drawings depicted him with two wolves at his side. I couldn't help but think of the symbolism and connection with my rune-painting friend, Wolf.

To my surprise, multiple Internet pages attested to Odin being accompanied by an eight-legged flying horse named Sleipner. Nowhere in my schooling or personal studies had I ever learned about Odin or heard of his flying horse.

Even more astounding, I found multiple translations of an epic poem about Odin that described him hanging, wounded, from a great tree for nine nights after having been pierced by a spear. I gaped at a drawing of Odin with a spear protruding from the exact spot on his torso where I felt the piercing pain.

A few stanzas later, the poem described how Odin looked down while hanging from that ancient tree and "with a loud cry, took up runes." The drawing showed runelike stones strewn at the base of the tree. I had no idea that Odin was credited with their discovery until he declared that he would teach me the secrets of the runes.

I recalled then that he had instructed me to find a specific rune. A few clicks on my keyboard and I found a pictorial spread of the 24 runic symbols. The one shaped like a lightning bolt stood out quite clearly. The label beneath the drawing read "Ansuz." When I clicked the name and read the description, I shook my head in amazement.

Ansuz is known as "Odin's rune." It is the rune of messages, prophecy, and wisdom. I glanced down at my notes and reread Odin's message to me: "There is much wisdom there."

My mind buzzed with questions. I could have continued my research online, but I preferred to get the answers directly from Odin. I knew that if I held the strong intention to converse with him again and it served the greater good, Odin would come back.

I returned to my meditation room and set a pad of paper and pen on my lap. Using methods described in Part II of this book, I relaxed my mind and body. When I had achieved the desired state of expanded consciousness, I shifted my focus and invited Odin to come into my awareness.

Within seconds I felt lightheaded, and my mind's eye filled with images of the bearded man. His strong but benevolent presence put me at ease, and I sent a silent greeting from my heart.

If you are a teacher, I said silently, *please teach me about your world.*

Thoughts flowed in response, and I wrote them verbatim: *We do not wear robes or have bodies and faces. We are concepts, patterns, fashioned in a form you would recognize. It is a convenience for Consciousness to take form.*

The words made sense but raised even more questions. Feeling quite bewildered, I asked, *Were you* real?

He replied, *As real as you are but not human.*

I paused to digest this response. By then I understood about Awareness and experience as the foundation of all that exists. Odin need not have ever walked in physical form in our world to exist as exactly what he had shared: *concepts and patterns, fashioned in a form you would recognize.*

The challenge was I had always believed that myths were simply stories made up by humans to explain the world and its phenomena. Now I found myself having an interactive conversation with a sentient being who had shared accurate parts of his story that I knew nothing about. I expressed my confusion rather strongly, stating, *But you are a myth!*

And without missing a beat, Odin replied, *YOU are a myth.*

People often ask me how to know if the things they experience in meditation are real or their imagination. One of the prime ways is that the words and insights are fresh, new, and not what you would expect. That was quite clearly the case with Odin's surprising response.

His reply knocked my worldview on its end. At first I felt a bit defensive. What did he mean, "You are a myth?!" But after contemplating what I had previously learned from the higher realms, his words made great sense.

THE STORY OF YOU

In saying, "You are a myth," Odin was not implying, "You are not real." He is asking us to see our human lives for what they are: one limited aspect of our multidimensional experiences.

What is a story? It is a narrative that connects a stream of events. Is that not what this life is? You experience "being" as a continuous flow of ST-F . . . sensations, thoughts, and feelings that appear to be connected. And they are connected as "concepts and patterns, fashioned in a form you would recognize."

A myth is a story. Myths feature archetypes in the form of characters, situations, and events that appear repeatedly throughout different stories in diverse cultures. Myths, like all good stories, follow a similar storyline. The protagonist embarks on an adventure that leads him or her into the unknown. Along the way, the main character encounters challenges and temptations. He or she is helped by mentors or guides who gift them with insights and revelations. In the end, they experience triumph and transformation.

This popular pattern is known as "the hero's journey," and it is what your soul came here to experience. Your soul's journey plays out on the stage of planet Earth. Your costume is a human body. You chose this role and the other actors with whom you would interact. You agreed to the overall plot and to specific milestones within the story, but for much of it, the details are unscripted. You are free to choose your reactions and responses to every new experience. That's what makes it so exciting for the soul and you, the hero of this story.

The problems occur when you take your role so seriously that you forget your Higher Self. You allow the role to define who you are, identifying exclusively with the conditioned sensations, thoughts, and feelings that go with the part. This is like a method actor who begins to believe he or she is the character they are portraying. Unless you maintain soul awareness and step out of character every so often, suffering is a big part of the story.

ALL IS NOT AS IT SEEMS

Odin said he is "as real as you are but not human." If I had dismissed his visits as "not real," I would have denied myself his third magical appearance. I hadn't thought of him in at least three months when he dropped in again during my daily meditation. Startled by his unexpected presence, I said nothing and waited to see why he had come.

He picked up where we left off, saying, *You must stop differentiating between real and unreal. Do you not know now that angels and archetypes are real? All archetypes are groupings of consciousness at different levels of vibration. Anything that you can create in consciousness is real and can convey truth, messages, information, learning, healing, and growth. All is not as it seems. You are just another part of me.*

And there it was—the main point of his visits. He came to show that it doesn't matter if you label your experiences "real" or "unreal" or call them figments of your imagination. What matters is: Do they help you in your journey? Are your experiences helpful and healing?

In stating "you are just another part of me," he was speaking to the fundamental unity of all beings. We are all stories arising in the One Mind.

I thanked Odin for his wise counsel. He nodded and then turned the tables with an unexpected question for me: *Who was my son?*

He asked as if he knew I had the answer, and I did. I recalled this bit of trivia from my research the first time Odin appeared.

Your son was Thor, I replied.

Yes, he nodded. *And who was your stepdaughter's dog?*

My mind rewound to the last visit Ty and I enjoyed with Susan. We had no idea it was the last time we would see her in physical form. She introduced us then to her new puppy. She told us his name at the time, but with all the emotion of her passing six months later, I had forgotten about the dog.

I suddenly realized that Odin's question about Susan's puppy was rhetorical. He asked it to help me remember that six months before Susan was struck and killed by lightning, she had named her new puppy Thor, after the Norse god of thunder and lightning.

And it took a visit by Thor's father, Odin, to help me make the connection.

Having made his point, Odin withdrew. I pulled myself back to waking consciousness and went in search of Ty. I found him at the bathroom sink, shaving.

"Ty, I just had a visit from Odin!" I reported.

My husband, one of the most logical, left-brained men I know, did not seem surprised. By now, he was used to my adventures in consciousness. They were always accompanied by verifiable information that I had no prior knowledge of, so he was completely on board with my journey.

"Really?" He set his razor on the counter and turned to me. "What did he say?"

I summarized Odin's revelation about Susan and her dog, knowing that Ty had also failed to make the connection between Susan's death by lightning and her having a dog named Thor.

We marveled together at yet another sign that the soul knows details about its impending transition that don't always filter into conscious awareness. As I turned to leave the bathroom, a subtle thought tickled my mind.

"Ty," I said, as goose bumps erupted on my arms, "what was Susan's other dog's name?"

He paused to think but could not remember.

I drew a blank as well. We stood there for a moment, struggling to recall, but I need not have tried. The answer was deposited in my awareness, no doubt from on high. An instant later, the name burst from my mouth: "Loki!"

"That's it," Ty confirmed.

"I remember reading that name," I said, pulling my iPhone from my pocket. Just as I had during Odin's first visit, I went to Google and typed in the four letters of "Loki." In an instant, my unspoken suspicions proved valid.

Loki was Odin's son.

It would be several years until I remembered that Susan had three dogs at the same time. The third was a female mixed breed that she named Athena. In yet another startling indicator of the intricacy of the web of connections, Susan had chosen the Greek goddess of thunder and lightning as her canine companion's name.

Some months later, it was Susan who put all the pieces of Odin's visit together for me in a most unexpected way. She appeared to me unbidden in meditation with her usual pleasant greeting. I could see her smile and hear her familiar lilting voice as she said, *Hey, Suzanne!*

What happened next met all the criteria of a not-my-imagination experience. It was fresh, new, and completely unexpected. One moment I was conversing with Susan, and in the next instant, her image faded and morphed quite seamlessly into Odin's.

As I struggled to make sense of this wispy role-swapping, a stream of words bubbled up in my awareness: *All is not as it seems. You are just another part of Me.*

The thoughts seemed to come from the bearded man before me, but this time I didn't make the mistake of attributing them to Odin. I knew the insights came from "This" . . . from Source-*being*-Joy expressing Itself temporarily through one of its patterns and concepts that humans call Odin.

The willingness to accept that all is not as it seems allowed me to see the strange experience anew: Joy-as-Suzanne had been greeted initially by Joy appearing as Susan. Then, because the entire experience was arising within the One Mind of Joy, Joy simply switched roles to become Odin.

As this realization arose and subsided into the vast sea of Awareness, Joy-as-Odin subsided and arose once again as Susan.

It's all malleable, Joy-as-Susan now explained. *You said you wanted to experience Oneness. It's all of us! We are all the same, just different instruments in one symphony! Whichever instrument you focus on is the one you experience.*

I pictured a concert hall and thought about the times I had sat in an audience and shifted my awareness for the diverse experiences this afforded. I could focus on a single musician or an entire section to pick out specific notes. I could choose to take in the music from the orchestra as a whole. Experiences like these demonstrate that Consciousness is indeed malleable.

With this magical morphing of very *real* characters, Joy was giving me the experience of unbounded awareness. Whether arising as Odin, as Susan, as you, as me, or as any grouping of Consciousness, Joy arises as a harmonious symphony of players in multiple realities.

Joy expresses itself throughout various realities as patterns of consciousness. In the lineage that produces the human story, Joy arises as what we call souls. These "fields of Joy-as-Spacious Awareness" choose human roles as ways to experience Joy-as-souls-in-a-body. Human roles are greatly limited compared to unbounded Wholeness, but they appear as fascinating archetypes: the warrior, the sage, the caregiver, the lover, and many more.

I continued my musing until Joy-as-Susan interrupted me with a question: *Now can "you" move away from center stage? That's the whole point. You can play any of these roles, because it's all God/Joy, and the more you surrender, the greater the connection and the Power.*

As I returned to full waking consciousness, I struggled at first to make sense of the unexpected experience. Remembering how Susan morphed into Odin and then back into Susan, I couldn't help but wonder, *Were the visits by Odin all just Susan showing up in disguise?* I had felt their unique personalities, and Odin showed me many things I couldn't have known.

And then Higher Consciousness pulled me out of my limited human thinking to remind me: "All is not as it seems. You are just another part of Me."

The experience was real. It was both Susan and Odin and also Joy showing up in the perfect way at the perfect time to deliver the perfect message: the basic essence of life is undivided wholeness.

Unmodified *being* arises as experiences in the One Mind. Over time, these experiences in Awareness become recognizable patterns containing all the attributes of their

Source: intelligence, creativity, self-awareness. The patterns flow and become narratives . . . stories.

The All is in the small and the small is in the All. There is only One Mind, and thus, everything is connected.

Picture the greater reality like the fabled Indra's net, a vast web with a jewel at each juncture. Each jewel represents an individual life form, or unit of consciousness, like the soul. Each jewel reflects all the others in a vast cosmic matrix.

Awareness had bubbled up in my meditation as Odin for the joy of helping other role-players awaken from the illusion that they could possibly be separate from Joy.

Joy-as-Susan used the analogy of a symphony when she came with her message of Oneness, and it is a most fitting one: *Which instrument you focus upon is the one you experience.*

You are Joy playing the role of a soul playing the role of a human being.

With awareness, you can cross the threshold and complete the Hero's Journey, safe in the awareness that Joy will show up exactly as needed, when needed, and you cannot ever be alone.

POINT OF VIEW
IS EVERYTHING

———

What do you do when the world gets you down?
You realize this is not the only world.
This-Awareness makes all the difference in the world.

— Sanaya

You know how it is in a theater when the movie ends. People either head straight for the exit or make a bee-line for the restroom. I chose the latter one evening after attending a lighthearted but rather unremarkable film. For a few minutes, I had the 10-stall ladies' room to myself.

And then, the blockbuster in the next theater let out. I stood at the sink washing my hands when a group of women who looked like they had just attended a funeral paraded in. Usually, in such circumstances, women chatter excitedly, comparing thoughts about the movie they just watched. In this case, no one said a word. A pall of depression hung in the air like acrid smoke.

Stunned by the gloomy aura that now filled the restroom, I asked the woman closest to me, "What movie did you just see?"

She exhaled her reply: "*American Sniper.*"

I shook my head as I returned to the lobby. I couldn't understand why anyone would willingly pay for an experience that left them so miserable. I had fully intended to see the movie at some point, but after experiencing the depressive effect it had on those in attendance, I had second thoughts.

And then, an insight bubbled up. My friend Lynette and I often joke about our souls sitting in the balcony of a theater watching ourselves in our human suits do silly things on the stage. We imagine one of our souls saying, "Oh, no! She's not going to do that, is she?" And the other soul shakes her head and says warily, "I think she might."

"Don't do it!" both souls shout. And then, our two souls lean in for a closer look, munching mindlessly on popcorn. We groan as our human characters continue an unmistakable path toward some common human blunder, knowing all is well no matter what. Still, we moan, "Oh, man, this one's going to hurt!"

While we use this scenario to make light of life, we both know it may not be too far from the truth. Having spent time in expanded meditative states, we have no doubt there is a part of us that is unaffected by our human roles.

When one of us is going through a rough patch, we don't tell the other not to be sad or upset. We acknowledge our human challenges as very real. And then we give a knowing smile and say with great compassion, "Pass the popcorn."

This puts everything in perspective.

I wondered if I could attend *American Sniper* with the goal of not getting caught up in the drama. What if I sat through the movie not as entertainment but as an experiment in practicing the Objective Observer perspective of the soul?

With this intriguing challenge in mind, I returned to the cinema one week later. As the action on the screen became more intense, I shifted to Observer mode. I kept myself from getting sucked into the drama by mentally repeating phrases such as, *This is a movie* and *These are actors*. I remained emotionally neutral by stating, *Isn't that interesting?* when something that would normally upset me happened in the script.

These conscious choices turned a cinematic experience into a sociological study. Without labeling the players "good guys" and "bad guys," I viewed the characters on both sides of the conflict without judgment and saw them with greater compassion. I realized how and why each made the choices they did. I didn't agree with or approve of many of the actions playing out on the screen, but I understood why they occurred.

The movie ends with a tragedy for the protagonist that you don't see coming. I realized why most people left the theater so subdued. For me, the experiment proved successful. I walked out in the same state of mind as I entered, and I gained valuable insights about human nature that are worth far more than the price of admission.

LIVING CONSCIOUSLY

If you're like most people, you don't go to movies to engage in a clinical study of human behavior. You go to be entertained. Movies provide a safe environment to feel the heightened emotions that make you feel most alive. You willingly subject yourself to high drama knowing you can avert your eyes like my friend Irene did during the tense scenes in *Top Gun*. If a movie is too stressful, you simply walk out of the theater.

Yes, you can opt out of the human experience intentionally, but this is not recommended. Like the moviegoer, you, the soul, took on this role for the heightened emotions you can experience while in human form. Nonphysical beings don't encounter extremes of happy and sad, peaceful and angry. They don't feel shame or unworthiness. They don't rage or cry with grief.

When dealing with these oh-so-human experiences, you may protest, "I never would have signed up for this!" And yet, at the soul level, you did, for the tremendous growth opportunities that such extremes present.

From the human perspective, there is a certain attraction to drama, both positive and negative. But "real life" can seem overwhelming if you can't avert your eyes or leave the theater. The liberating piece of the movie analogy is stated perfectly in the quote from Sanaya at the beginning of this chapter: "What do you do when the world gets you down? You realize this is not the only world."

Awareness of your multidimensional nature allows you to choose your perspective moment by moment. The choices include:

- Experiencing life from the human point of view, getting completely caught up in the storyline

- Maintaining the neutral, detached, yet compassionate perspective of the soul throughout any challenging situation

- Shifting from the human perspective to that of the soul as circumstances dictate

Can you feel the freedom afforded by consciously choosing your point of view? You are not stuck in your story. You can step out of the role at any time and assume the Observer's perspective. To do so brings relief, peace, and insights on how to act when you step back onto the stage.

Living The Awakened Way does not mean your life is boring or devoid of emotions. On the contrary. By living consciously, you can fearlessly take on greater adventures knowing there is a safety valve: a simple shift to the soul's perspective where peace reigns.

Any challenge you face is easier to handle when you shift to soul mode. The diagram below illustrates how this dual nature as Experiencer and Observer can co-exist. If you focus on the white parts, you see two faces. If you shift your attention to the black part in the center, you see a vase.

This diagram does not contain either two faces or a vase. It contains both. You are not either a soul or a human. You are both, and also the wholeness of the entire expression of being.

Keep in mind that the diagram represents a visual shift. Changing perspective from the human point of view to the soul's much more objective viewpoint is a mental activity.

One of the limitations of being in physical form is that you can only hold the soul's perspective for brief periods. To better understand this, look at the vase–face picture again and try to hold your awareness of both images at the same time. Because of how the brain functions, you can do so briefly, followed by a shuttling back and forth that quickly becomes tiresome.

Likewise, the soul is your essential nature. You are always present as the soul—but it takes awareness and intention to shift from conditioned human ways of being to your more expanded state.

Meditation and other techniques that you will learn in Part II allow you to hold soul awareness for extended periods. With intention and practice, you can become quite skillful at shining your inner light more often and more brightly.

Despite appearances, the soul and your human nature are not physical objects like a vase or a face. Each is a state of being arising in the One Mind of Awareness. "Human" and "soul" are not fixed but are flowing states. Each arises along an expanding spectrum of nested states of awareness from limited to limitless. For simplicity's sake, let's call the human aspect "limited awareness" and the soul "spacious awareness." Ultimately, there is only one Soul, one state of "being" from which all that exists arises.

You, as pure Awareness in expression, are constantly shifting between these limited/spacious states. The times when you judge others or may say unkind things indicate you are in "fully human" mode. Blissful moments when you feel at one with all that is indicate you have upgraded to soul awareness. Awakened people hold spacious awareness as often as possible and notice when they have slipped into limited awareness.

Don't fall into the trap of thinking you must achieve perfection to come to know your highest nature. Your more limited aspects are all part of Joy. It's simply more obvious who and what you are when you align your thoughts and actions with Love.

What a joy it is to realize you are not confined by the limitations of life in a body! You never have been, except by a case of mistaken identity.

As a beautiful, shining soul, you are free to observe and flow with each experience. You signed up for the fullness of this earthly experience. When emotions and the drama of being human get to be a bit much, take a breath, sit back for a moment, and pass the popcorn.

YOU ARE
NEVER ALONE

———

The way you gaze upon a newborn babe? That is how Source gazes
upon you. The way you cannot get enough of a delicious scent? That
is how desirable your life is to Spirit. The way you think "how clever"
when a child recites the alphabet? That is the joy Joy feels at your
growth. Do not think you stand alone and ignored. Do not think you
do not matter. Do not think at all when it comes to your worth. Go
to the heart where the soul knows. You are so very loved.

— Sanaya

Your soul agreed to take on this life you're living. You
knew it would be filled with great challenges but also with
the potential for great joy. Saying yes to this adventure
was easier because you knew that help would always be
available. Of course, life on earth becomes more difficult when you forget that your nonphysical helpers are
always with you.

You know your spirit team quite well at the soul level.
Like the hair on your head, they are such an integral

part of your normal energy field that you may not notice their presence.

Guides do their best to keep you safe and to keep your life flowing smoothly. You have at least one main spirit guide who is with you from your first breath to your last. Others come and go throughout your life to help with specific issues such as challenges with work, creativity, family, finances, maintaining emotional balance, and so forth.

Guides are instantly accessible and communicate in a variety of ways. They put thoughts in your mind to help you make critical decisions. They nudge you to notice things that will make your journey easier. They use synchronicity to show that you are being helped. You may hear a clear voice in your head or be filled with a sense of knowing that you're supposed to take a specific action. Whether you feel their presence or not, trust that they are here.

After I began to communicate with loved ones who have passed, I resisted the idea of spirit guides. The concept of heavenly helpers seemed like something out of a fairy tale. Now I'm grateful for my nonphysical team's persistence in proving their presence because I can't imagine life without them.

My most unforgettable interaction with my main guide, Boris, occurred while on our annual Messages of Hope tour around the United States. Ty and I were enjoying a quiet evening in our RV, and I decided it was time to break out a new book from a stack I had brought along. I reached into the cabinet overhead and chose one that looked interesting.

Quite unexpectedly, I heard my guide Boris's voice in my mind.

Not that one, he said.

I frowned and sent back a silent reply. *But I want to read this one.*

Choose the one on the bottom, he said.

If there's one thing I've learned in my interactions with guides it's this: You can push back when you get a helpful heavenly message. Push back a second time, and you may well regret it.

I gave a wry laugh and swapped my choice of book for the one on the bottom.

Settling in on the sofa, I opened the cover and began to scan the fore pages.

Turn to the back, Boris directed.

I dutifully turned the book over and scanned the jacket. Nothing stood out.

Look inside *the back cover.*

Never had I received such clear, step-by-step guidance. With growing excitement and curiosity, I opened the hardcover from the back and gasped in surprise. The book was one of nine I bought prior to our trip. It had sat in the cabinet, never opened, for the two months we had been on the road. Now I gazed upon a picture of a landscape that Ty and I had photographed that very day. The synchronicity floored me.

Below the photo of the iconic scene, I noted an advertisement for a spiritual retreat center I had never heard of. Reading the description, my skin erupted in goose bumps. It sounded like a place I would love to visit. At the very bottom of the page, I saw an address. I didn't recognize the town, but the state was just north of the one where we camped.

Ty did all the planning for our trips, so I looked up from the book and said, "Honey, which way are we headed tomorrow?"

"We're going north," he replied, and mentioned our day's destination.

I rose from the couch and pulled out a map covering the local area. Tracing a line from our current location to the next day's campground, I did a double take. We had traveled 2,500 miles on our tour to that point. The retreat center in the book Boris had guided me to was exactly 10 miles north of us on a secondary road. The route my husband had planned for the following day's travel would take us directly past it.

I shared the astounding discovery with Ty. We agreed that I had to visit the place.

Imagine my excitement the next morning when we pulled into the parking lot of the retreat center from the book Boris had guided me to! Ty went with me to the lobby, where a hostess greeted us pleasantly and offered us a tour.

Everything seemed quite normal at first, but with each step farther into the bowels of the complex, the discomfort in my gut grew. Ty, who is not normally sensitive to energy, shot me a few questioning glances at some of the unusual artwork, icons, and activities we witnessed around us.

After half an hour of ever-increasing strangeness, the lyrics of "Hotel California" began to play in my mind. True fear that we might not be allowed to leave rippled through me as the word *cult* flashed like a neon sign in my mind.

Our hostess invited us to stay in the sanctuary for as long as we cared to. Ty and I were quick to offer our regrets before making a hasty retreat for the nearest exit. The welcome glare of the bright sun shined in stark contrast to the dark feeling that lingered within. We scurried in stunned silence across the parking lot toward our RV.

"I don't understand this at all," I said to Ty as I slipped into the passenger seat. Boris had clearly led me here, and guidance from our nonphysical team members is always helpful and healing.

"That was creepy," he replied as he hastily cranked the engine to life.

"If you don't mind, I need to have a conversation with Boris."

"Go for it," he said, knowing I needed him to be silent while I meditated.

I took a few centering breaths and, using pure intention, shifted my focus to the level where we meet our guides.

Boris, I said silently, *you led me to that book knowing I would be going past that retreat center the next day. Why did you send me there? I didn't resonate with it at all.*

The answer came immediately. *For the lessons.*

I sent him a wordless question in response. His answer came in full sentences:

Now you have no doubt that we know precisely where you are, what you are doing, and where you are going every moment. It can be no other way, for all is connected. In addition to this most important lesson, we wanted to bring attention to the fact that your reading list could easily take you off track.

I frowned and ran through the titles of the books I had brought on the trip. In truth, several of them dealt with esoteric metaphysical topics that some might consider a bit "out there."

Is the information in them incorrect? I asked Boris.

This is not the issue, he replied. *The heart is your best judge with any new teaching. The issue is that your soul's task is to help a more mainstream audience understand and connect to Higher Consciousness. Stick to the basics and teach only love.*

And with that, he withdrew, leaving me humbled by the message.

That afternoon when we settled in at our next campsite, I sorted through the remaining books in the cabinet over the couch. I picked up each one and gave it the heart test. The books that failed the test by giving me a tightness in my chest and solar plexus went into a large green garbage bag.

Even though all the books were brand-new, I took that bag directly to the nearest dumpster. In the days that followed, I never doubted my decision to discard them.

I also never again doubted the existence of guides.

How would your life have unfolded if you had known you have ever-present helpers? Before I came to know this truth, I stayed in an unhealthy relationship far too long. I couldn't stand the thought of being alone. I struggled to make big decisions because I didn't trust myself. I did things I regretted because I thought it was me against the world.

Don't beat yourself up if you've been in the same boat. Look to the past only to learn. You can establish a relationship with your team of helpers starting immediately. Begin to call on them regularly and experience the difference that working with your guides makes.

You may be wondering why your guides haven't helped you more as you've struggled with life's challenges. They have helped you more than you may realize. You can live your entire life without ever acknowledging your ever-present helpers. When you work with them consciously, however, the difference is stunning.

Do you want your guides' specific help and clear advice? Simply ask. That's how it works. They may not have all the answers, but their perspective is naturally higher than yours while you're in a body.

Be aware that your guides can't take away your suffering. Only you can do that by remaining aware of your thoughts and not identifying solely with the elements of your story. They can help you to remember to live lucidly, however. Set the intention that they will nudge you in a way that you notice when you're wandering off track.

Guides love to cooperate with you. Taking care of you is their job, and they love you. They learn and grow from helping you as much as you learn from them. And don't forget to thank them often. They appreciate when you acknowledge their presence and their assistance.

Believe. Trust. Play. Call them guides, call them angels, call them higher beings. It doesn't matter what you call them—just call them.

LIFE IS LOVE IN FULL EXPRESSION

Out beyond ideas of right-doing and wrong-doing,
there is a field. I will meet you there.

— Rumi

There is a natural tendency in life to flow toward wholeness. Witness the following examples:

- Do re mi fa sol la ti

- What goes up must

- Eight plus six equals fourt____

There is a part of you that simply must complete whatever is incomplete. You can sense this urge in the physical body. Go back and read the three phrases again, but this time pay attention to your midsection as you do so.

The subtle clenching that accompanies a lack of wholeness is like what you experience when leaning forward at the edge of a drop-off. Stress and tension are the natural response

69

to imbalance of any kind, be it physical, mental, emotional, or spiritual. You innately sense that something is missing.

Life is one complete energetic whole in ever-changing states of unfolding and enfolding. It is a process, an eternal flow, a dynamic dance of being and becoming. What is empty seeks to be filled. What is filled to overflowing seeks release.

If you're like most humans, you walk around in a state of imbalance without realizing it. Your human nature pays homage to the logical left brain. Meanwhile, the soul's intuitive gifts languish in the underused right lobe. Ignoring your wholeness and favoring head over heart manifests as a near-constant teetering-at-the-edge feeling.

Until you learn to feed the soul, you may seek relief by feeding your physical desires. Such pursuits can be enjoyable when the choice to engage in them is conscious and moderated. Problems occur when moderation turns into addictive behavior that numbs your human awareness even more than its already limited state.

The soul knows what you need to feel good in any moment. It will naturally guide you to balance if you check in instead of checking out. Granted, this earthly boarding school is not for the faint of heart, but you knew that when you enrolled, brave soul.

I remember feeling mentally and physically drained one Monday morning after teaching a weekend workshop. The human side of me wanted to crawl back into bed after breakfast. A little voice inside nudged me to ignore my human desires and gift myself with movement and fresh air.

I chose to go for a bike ride in a beautiful wooded area near our house. Most of the trails in this popular mountain biking complex are beginner level. They are flat and covered with a soft bed of pine needles, providing a smooth, flowy experience that riders refer to as "buttery."

Honoring my depleted state, my husband set a reasonable pace as we started out. I followed behind him, smiling as we glided through the gentle S-curves and floated over the occasional "whoop-de-doos"—rounded bumps that give the stomach a fun little lurch.

The ride was a balm for my soul. I enjoyed half an hour of soaking up the energy of the sun and trees, unaware that the green blazes marking the beginner trail had changed to swaths of blue. This color is used to indicate more technical sections of the complex. "Technical" is mountain bike lingo for "filled with gnarly obstacles" that could result in what riders refer to as a "face-plant."

The crunch of gravel replaced the swish of pine straw, and I began fishtailing through the curves. As my bike's fat tires ran into roots and rocks of varying sizes, my smile morphed into a thin-lipped scowl. I clenched my teeth and gripped the handlebars.

A mountain bike is made to glide over obstacles. If you allow it to do its job instead of trying to control it, the bike will carry you quite well to your destination. Clenching and gripping are not good form. Just like in life, the harder you hold on, the rougher the ride.

Finally, after one too many jarring full-body shocks, I growled aloud, "This is supposed to be a relaxing ride!"

Instantly, a deep, booming voice bellowed back at me from the heavens: *It's a mountain bike trail, for God's sake!*

This inner retort was so unexpected and so comically profound that I burst into laughter.

The Source of that voice had made its point quite clear: roots and rocks are a natural part of riding in the woods. I had willingly made the choice to get on the bike. My intention was to enjoy an easy ride, but I took a few unexpected turns. To become upset by a ride that includes both smooth and rough patches shows a lack of awareness and acceptance of the nature of mountain biking.

The insight instantly changed my mood. I saw myself through the soul's eyes and couldn't help but laugh at my human demands that life conform to my desires and always be pleasant.

When we get caught up in the story, we could all use a booming voice to remind us, *It's Earth School, for God's sake!*

Life in a physical body is not always buttery. There are plenty of technical sections filled with obstacles. You, the soul, chose to take on this well-known journey with its ups and downs and unexpected obstacles. *To become upset by experiences that include both smooth and rough patches shows a lack of awareness of the nature of this reality and your reason for incarnating.*

Earth School is not a reform school. You did not come here to learn your lessons because anything is lacking. This is a human-innovation laboratory for the spacious awareness of the soul, which is already whole and complete.

You came here to enjoy the fullness of the creative experience. In the process, any growth you experience adds to the growth of humanity as a whole.

What better way could there be for humans to evolve than in an environment of trial and error, where free will stretches and pulls against rigid rules? This creative tension results in an inner urge to progress ever onward, ever upward through winding curves and over the occasional whoop-de-doos.

You, the soul, arise from the boundless potential of pure *Being.* Moment by moment the Absolute is bursting with creativity that simply must be expressed, and you are the result.

Artists, composers, and writers know the irrepressible impulse that bubbles and percolates, churns and gurgles until they absolutely must mold thoughts and ideas into manifest creations.

As above, so below.

At the soul level, you made the conscious choice to funnel your creative potential into a body. The brain, heart, nervous system, and earthly environment provide limitless opportunities for the soul that are not possible in your formless state.

You, the soul, can use your amazing body to fling paint at a blank canvas; to sing off-key at the top of your lungs; to dance barefoot in the moonlight; and to cut, carve, and compose, taking ideas and concepts and creating something more beautiful from what has already been birthed in Awareness.

Unlike in other realms, it is here in Earth School that you get to roll around in every imaginable pair of opposites. In this creative arts workshop, you are given a palette that includes all possible colors. As any artist learns, it is the skillful use of contrast that takes an ordinary scene and transforms it into a masterpiece.

Darkness and shadow—the roots and rocks of this unpredictable ride—are inherently part of life in the physical dimension. As the Light shines upon the objective world, its opposite naturally results.

It's understandable that you may want off the planet when your sole identity is the elements of your earthly story with its inherent ups and downs. You will instinctively turn to the kind of mind-numbing behaviors mentioned above until you discover there is a better way to deal with the disconnect between expectations and experience.

That better way is The Awakened Way of balancing soul awareness with human nature. Instead of demanding that life go the way you want it, you flow with what is.

You realize that all arises from one indivisible field, one Wholeness. Nothing is left out.

This is the true definition of Love, and it is why many say that God is Love. This Wholeness is connection, completion, the expression of the totality in its limitless parts and watching how they all fumble and finally fit together.

When you flow with what life puts in your path, you take in every bit of it, bumps and all. In allowing the entirety of what presents itself, fullness replaces the emptiness. Disappointments, failure, rejections—all are part of a tapestry that no longer has holes in it. Instead, the bright spots woven into your story stand out, as if spotlighted.

No one escapes Earth School without scrapes and bruises, yet your wounds hold the key to your transformation. Your discomfort is the soul's prompting to recognize the light within you and shine it outward, no matter what. When you do so, you find what you've unwittingly been looking for all along: wholeness.

Let there be no doubt: you arrived in physical form with full awareness of your Divinity with no blocks to your creative flow. Before you developed a story and the resultant ego co-opted the left side of your brain, the flowy right hemisphere ruled your actions. Give a child a coloring book with an assortment of finger paints, and you will see Joy in action.

You can regain this childlike, creative, flowing state. It hasn't gone away. You simply need to start choosing brighter colors from your box of crayons and draw outside the lines as Spirit moves you.

The soul has no "shoulds," "musts," or "have-tos." It doesn't need rules because it knows only connection and flows with what is. It wants you to know that you have great reason to love life and wake up excited about the day ahead. The soul wants you to celebrate the promise that:

- You are not only human. You are a unique expression of the one Divine Mind.

- There is no death, only endings and beginnings of chapters in the eternal Journey of Awareness.

- Every experience is temporary. "This too shall pass" is a phrase worth repeating when the story gets a bit dramatic.

- At the deepest level, there is nothing to fear precisely because everything is temporary and there is no death.

- You are never alone, because you and beings at all levels are the expression of the same Source.

- In serving and connecting with others, you find your innate connection with all that is.

- Help is as close as your breath because it is the Life Force that breathes you. Breathe, relax, and reach out for assistance.

- You are not judged for your mistakes. Each moment is a new beginning. Vow to consider what appear to be missteps, make better choices next time, and move onward, knowing . . .

- You are cherished beyond measure, no matter what.

The soul wants you to know that you came here to be fully human for the hell of it and the joy of it. Challenges come with the costume, but oh, the fullness that awaits you now as you remember that the human part and the soul cannot be separated from the whole.

In no longer resisting or rejecting the darkness and shadows, life magically reveals itself as LIFE: love in *full* expression.

Stop gripping the handlebars when rocks turn up in your path. It's well known among mountain bikers that if you stare at an obstacle, you will run right into it. Breathe, relax, and make the conscious, awakened choice to *BE* with every experience and emotion that arises. In so doing, you cannot help but enjoy a wondrous state of flow.

This is Wholeness.

From this moment forward, whenever you feel stressed, depressed, or any other of the many fully human attributes that are guaranteed to show up in the human experience, instead of numbing your awareness, pause, breathe deeply, and flow.

You, beautiful soul, will notice the surface disturbances, yet in this state of Wholeness, you will also be aware of absolute stillness . . . the peace that remains undisturbed in the depths of your being.

No longer will people need to act a certain way for you to be happy. No longer will life need to unfold according to an idealized and unrealistic human idea of the perfect world. Emptiness will be a thing of the past, eclipsed by fullness.

This is LIFE: love in full expression.

Feel the soul rejoicing that you are finally doing what you came here to do: to experience *everything* that life in a body has to offer but now from a higher perspective.

The Story of You is not a fairy tale. It is real. It is messy. And it is Divine, as only unique and beautiful *you* could enable Joy to experience it.

PART II

THE
PRACTICES

PREFACE TO PART II

Having read the preceding chapters, you now have a basic understanding about reality beyond your human story and who you are at the deeper levels. No amount of reading, however, can substitute for the actual experience of your multidimensional nature. In this section, you will learn tools to visit this state without having to travel at all.

The goal of every activity in this book is to help you live The Awakened Way, consciously engaging with your own Higher Self and intelligent, creative, nonphysical beings who have your best interests at heart. Once you begin to shift your focus from the objective physical world at will, you will be able to enjoy wondrous, insightful, and transformational adventures in consciousness.

I personally use each of the practices you will learn here on a regular basis. I assure you that these tools and techniques hold the power to completely transform your life.

These are not exercises that you try one time and never do again. On the contrary, they will hopefully become a way of life once you see how useful they are in expanding your perspective and keeping ego and the human drama at bay.

Happily, they are easy to do anytime to clear away your conditioned human ways of thinking and acting. Over time, as you integrate these practices into your daily life, the results will be greater peace, joy, happiness, and compassion for yourself and your fellow human beings.

You may find that the impact and depth of your experiences with these practices change as you use them. If you set one aside for a time, pick it up again a few weeks or months later. The results can be both surprising and enriching as your understanding and connection with Spirit evolves.

To that end, Part II is divided into six sections. Each has several unique experiential practices for the specific issues, which include:

1. Getting to know your true nature

2. Maintaining a clear energy field

3. Making the connection with Higher Consciousness

4. Working with your Team in Spirit

5. Practicing presence

6. Coming into alignment with your true nature

No section or exercise is any more important than another. There is no specific order in which to practice what you learn. All the tools will help you to clear the clouds of human conditioning and reveal the clear sky of your spacious nature that is always and already present.

You may notice that in Part II, I repeatedly review some of the fundamental concepts about your true nature. The repetition is intentional. After a lifetime of thinking you are only human, it is important to completely integrate any new information into your belief system. Approaching the same concepts from multiple angles will mean they eventually take hold in your conscious awareness.

I have carefully spelled out the step-by-step instructions to the practices you will find here. They aren't complicated, nor do any of them require large investments of your time. I recognize that time is a precious commodity these days, but oh, the joys that await you when you discover the state beyond time that is yours for the taking!

Approach each exercise with a childlike sense of excitement and wonder, as in, "I wonder what awesome experiences will result from my efforts?" Be aware of any assumptions or expectations you are bringing to the experience and be willing to set these aside. Trust Spirit that your greatest good will be served as a result of your efforts.

Until this point in the book, your task has mainly been to read and digest what's written. That is about to change, as are you.

Please don't just read the instructions to the exercises that follow. Do the work. Results will follow, without fail. And after time, it won't feel like work at all. It will be your Joy, moment by moment, to take what you've learned and easily step into the fullness of *being*.

GETTING TO KNOW YOUR TRUE NATURE

Humans are creatures of habit. The story changes little day-to-day.

If you're like most people, you get out of bed and go through the same routine each morning with variations on the weekends. When new experiences arise in the storyline, you unconsciously search your memory for similar situations. If you find a match, you deal with the present issue, much like you did in the past, reenacting what is familiar and comfortable.

Getting to know your true nature asks you to step outside the story. It requires effort and making conscious choices to make the quantum leap to new ways of thinking and acting.

The practices in this first section are designed to help you know and notice the difference between your human traits and those of the soul. Here you will learn to question reality and make room for more expanded ways of perceiving your experiences.

These practices will help you to see your story and that of others from a higher perspective. The exercises may test your worldview a bit, but they're supposed to.

A wise teacher once told me, "If you're not making people squirm, you're not doing your job."

Note that there is a big difference between growing pains and fear. Take one step at a time as your human beliefs evolve. Test everything in the heart and never do anything that you feel would be harmful or hurtful.

Remember always that you are a direct expression of the one Light of Consciousness . . . of God. With this as your deepest truth, nothing can harm the soul.

So, if I've done my job right, you may feel a bit uncomfortable as you question your cherished beliefs, and that's a good thing. Only by stretching do you grow.

Semper Gumby![4]

---

4   "Always flexible." I include this expression in honor of my stepdaughter, Sergeant Susan Marie Giesemann-Babich, USMC. It is an oft-used phrase in the military as a play on the shortened form of the Marines' motto, "semper fi" (always faithful).

PRACTICE:
QUESTIONING WHAT IS

———

It's easy to take what you call "reality" for granted. You willingly accept certain statements about the way the world operates based on appearances, even when you know they're not true. Does the sun really rise and fall? Is your body solid, or is it a swirling pattern of information and energy at a deeper level? Could it be both?

Imagine if explorers in the age of Magellan had believed that the world is flat! By Questioning What Is, you uncover a reality beyond appearances and learn to navigate your experiences in Earth School with far less fear.

You seriously limit your growth by not questioning what you learn from other humans. Granted, it's not always comfortable to question "higher-ups," such as parents, teachers, preachers, and bosses. You can see evidence of the tendency to accept a belief system without question in the way most children adopt the same religion and political party as their parents.

The soul will do its best to nudge you when your beliefs are no longer in alignment with higher truths. It communicates quite clearly using body language, but you must be aware to notice the signals. Dissonance manifests as discomfort in the gut and heart. You may experience restlessness and a knowing that what you've been told just doesn't sit right anymore.

Rather than ignoring or sedating these feelings, be curious. Questioning What Is might not change your truth at the human level, but it may very well provide you an alternate understanding from the soul's perspective.

For example, from the human perspective, you would say, "Death is real." When you shift to the soul's point of view and experience very real connections with those who have passed, you come to understand, "There is no death."

Both statements are true, depending on your point of view. This expansion of your limited human beliefs leads to freedom from suffering.

It's in your best interest to gain information about any issue from the highest level possible. Questioning What Is does not entail directly questioning others. This is a personal, internal practice of investigation and contemplation.

Examples of the type of questions you might investigate include:

- What is the nature of God? (Is there a man on a cloud who doles out favors based on behavior or does all creation arise from "that beyond which there is nothing else"?)

- Do you have to believe certain things to gain access to the afterlife?

- Are all human beings worthy of love? (Can you see how the human perspective and that of the soul might differ in their response to this important question?)

- Is this life all there is?

- Who am I?

This last one is the most important question you can ask as you move toward True Self knowledge. You will want to ask this not just once but at regular intervals as your beliefs evolve. The insights you receive will change as your understanding of the Greater Reality expands.

This practice of asking "Who am I?" and contemplating the type of questions in the list above is called *self-inquiry*. You don't want to pose these deep questions the same way you might ask a friend, "How's the weather?" Questioning What Is comes from the soul level, beyond the story. This requires being open to your higher nature and shifting your point of view before you ask the questions.

Do not miss this important point!

Let's do a little self-inquiry now to show you how it works. Read through the following instructions and then do the practice:

- Close your eyes.

- With the goal of centering your attention fully on the task, take a slow, deep breath, inhaling to the count of four and exhaling to the count of six.

- Move your awareness to the area of your heart, the energetic connection point between human and soul awareness.

- Hold the intention of receiving an insightful answer, and ask the question: *How would I have answered "Who am I?" before I read the material in this book?*

- Sit quietly and notice what responses arise. You may choose to open your eyes and write them down or simply make a mental note of the insights received.

- Now ask the question, *What is my understanding in this moment of who I am?*

- Focus your attention on the responses that arise. Write the answers or simply make a mental note of them.

- Hold in awareness how your answers may continue to evolve as your understanding of reality expands.

- Set the intention to ask "Who am I?" regularly as your journey progresses.

- Give gratitude for any insights gained and open your eyes.

Notice how this practice requires you to first become centered. Taking one slow, relaxing breath and shifting your awareness to the heart is all it takes to align with the deeper part of you that is always and already here.

You can have a topic in mind each time you practice self-inquiry or see what issue arises spontaneously. There's no need to concern yourself with who is providing the answer. Future practices in this book will help you come to know some of the myriad expressions of Joy who may show up to answer your questions.

Be forewarned: Ego—the part of your story that needs acceptance and approval to survive—will want you to stick to the storyline. It will remind you that it's not good to question authority.

This begs the question: To which Authority will you answer? The ego or Higher Awareness?

Ego will want to make you think this authority figure is outside of yourself. By questioning your belief system moment by moment about who and what you are, you will put the bossy aspect of ego in its place, but please do so with love. You came here for the human experience and all that entails.

You may find that as your beliefs change, your inner circle will as well. Friends may naturally drift away, but you will come to realize this is okay because you no longer resonate with them. You'll find you can release them with love and without judgment as you are, over time, drawn to those whose beliefs and interests are more in alignment with your new way of thinking and being.

As for family members, the inner journey is unique to each person. Know that you can change your world-view while still honoring their thought systems. You do not have to think like them to love them at the soul level. As you progress in your understanding and expanding awareness, you'll find great peace in recognizing that each individual is here for their own experiences.

In the meantime, set the intention to notice when concepts you have learned from other humans no longer resonate in your heart. Investigate what makes you uncomfortable, and in that moment of awareness, may you discover the doorway to freedom.

You cannot possibly experience the fullness of who you really are while in a physical body. That is by design. Nevertheless, as you diligently question reality, your awareness of your multidimensional nature will increase. Through your ongoing efforts to learn and grow, your concept of how you fit into the Big Picture will grow with you.

PRACTICE:
SETTING THE STORY ASIDE

What you call "my life" is most definitely yours. It is also part of the cumulative experience of "The One," *being you.*

When you, (state your name), believe that your name and the elements that make up your story are your one and only self, you fail to see what is always and already here.

The highest part of you is that which is shared by all beings. Any practice that helps you to personally experience this shared, unified, indivisible state of being requires setting aside the contents of The Story of You.

Setting the Story Aside is an exercise you can do in just a few minutes with profound results. I recommend you do it often, most especially when peace seems hard to find.

Be aware that sensations, thoughts, and feelings will continue to arise within Aware Awareness as you spend moments experiencing the Absolute. What makes the practice of Setting the Story Aside so helpful in getting to know your true nature is an all-important shift in focus. You may be aware of ST-F bubbling up, but your attention remains fully on the purity of the no-thingness in which the ST-F appears.

Having shifted your focus from the doings, happenings, and arisings, you intentionally seek the opposite. You notice silence in the space between two thoughts. You glimpse the clean canvas in the pause between two images. You sense the cessation of drama between two emotions. You allow your awareness to rest in these nondoings, these nonhappenings, these pure *being* experiences that are right here, right now within you, where they have always been.

This is Home base.

In spending human time in these timeless moments of noticeable contrast, you become aware of the flow of life itself. This shift in focus from without to within transforms what you have taken for granted. You come to know that this silent stillness is the seed from which all life sprouts.

Setting the Story Aside is quite simple:

- Set the clear intention to spend a few minutes getting to know your True Self.

- Clear any distractions around you and get comfortable.

- Close your eyes and become centered with a few deep breaths.

- Actively seek the space and silence that fills all Awareness.

- Notice any sensations, thoughts, and feelings (ST-F) that arise and do not resist them.

- Return continuously to seeking the space and silence, observing how the ST-F naturally fades away.

- Ask yourself, "Who am I beyond the ST-F that makes up my story?"

- Notice fresh insights that arise within the ST-F.

- Give gratitude for what you have experienced and return to full waking consciousness.

The vastness you experienced, no matter how briefly, is the underlying essence of all life. It is both empty and full at the same time. It is the alpha and the omega—the starting point and end point of all the elements of every story and the entirety of every story, itself.

Don't become frustrated if you can't maintain your focus on this pure state of being for long periods. You aren't meant to while you're in a body. You came here for the human experience.

Life in Earth School can be quite challenging. Knowing *this* is here, now, always, is your relief valve. Lacking drama, this Source-Space becomes your haven, your respite, your go-to whenever the outer experience gets to be too much.

When you find yourself craving peace, practice Setting the Story Aside and enjoy a taste of Home.

THE JOY-US BEADS EXERCISE

Within minutes of meeting or observing someone from a distance, you form an opinion based on their appearance, speech, and mannerisms. Whether consciously or not, you size them up relative to your own story. Ultimately, people you encounter either attract or repel you.

Human beings learn and grow through relationships. Imagine how the world would change if instead of saying, "I don't like them," you would acknowledge what's really going on energetically and say, "I don't resonate with them."

Can you feel the difference between this statement and "I can't stand them"?

In recognizing a fundamental energetic difference instead of making things personal, you are acknowledging the human story and honoring the soul.

The soul does not judge. The soul is aware of the underlying unity of all beings.

You, the soul, came here to act out your unique human role for the experiences it offers. Yes, you could have decided to remain in nonphysical form and enjoy the peace that comes from maintaining unity consciousness. But you made a conscious choice to enroll in Earth School with all its challenges.

So, why bother seeing others with the eyes of the soul?

Because your human evolution depends upon it. Because your relationships require the soul's perspective to be successful. Because your joy and happiness are a direct result of looking beyond the surface and integrating soul awareness with your human role.

When you find yourself attracted to or repelled by someone, it is the human story and their energy field that you are reacting to. Happily, with intention, you can train yourself to break out of your "only human" perspective. You can choose to consciously gaze into the calm depths of every human with whom you interact and find your common Heritage.

I call this shared field of being "Joy." And oh, what a feeling it is to recognize Joy gazing back at you from behind the eyes of others! If you are to find joy in your life, you must first find Joy within yourself. If you are to find peace in your world, set the intention to find Joy in all that is.

What follows is a powerful practice to help you see all earthlings as not only fellow souls but also expressions of the one Source of all Being. This Force . . . this unique Joy . . . breathes through you and all others. Therefore, Joy is "We" and Joy is "Us."

This realization removes the sense of separation and division that dominates human behavior. To live in awareness of this deeper connection is indeed *joyous*, which is why I use a play on words by calling this next practice The Joy-Us Beads Exercise.

You will need to have a circular strand of beads in your hand. The circle is significant, as it is symbolic of the innate connection of all beings. You can use your grandmother's pearls or a homemade strand of beads strung together. A rosary or a set of mala beads will work just as well.

Read through the following instructions before doing the actual exercise:

- Sit quietly with the strand of beads in your nondominant hand.

- Close your eyes and become centered with several long, slow breaths.

- Move your awareness to the area of your heart, the energetic bridge between limited human awareness and the spacious awareness of the soul.

- Shift to soul awareness, affirming silently, "I am an expression of Joy, the Light of Awareness."

- Take your dominant hand and lightly grasp one bead between your thumb and index finger.

- Ask Joy to put into your mind a succession of people with whom you're familiar by name or title. They can be in physical form or across the veil. They can be people you have met or people you have only heard of. Examples include family members, friends, colleagues, employers, celebrities, politicians, and so forth.

- Note: The names and titles will vary each time you do this exercise. You do not have to "think up" any names or titles. By asking Higher Consciousness to help you, names will bubble up purposefully due to the emotions these particular names will arouse in you. Passively receiving the names versus trying to think of them provides excellent practice in remaining present, focused, and noticing fresh experiences arising from outside your normal conditioned thoughts.

- As a name or title arises in your mind, silently repeat the name followed by "is an expression of Joy." For example: "My mother is an expression of Joy."

- Notice how making this statement feels mentally, emotionally, and physically.

- Without opening your eyes, move your fingers to the next bead and await another name to arise in Awareness. As you hear it, repeat the process, silently filling in the blank with that name and stating (for example), "My friend John is an expression of Joy."

- Again, notice how it feels to claim that this person is an expression of Joy . . . Source . . . God.

- Continue moving to the next bead in the circle after receiving a name and affirming that this person is Joy in expression.

- Every few beads you may want to change "Joy" to other ways of referring to That Which Is Nameless, such as "Source," "Force," "God," "The All." (For example, "My boss is Source in expression.")

- Every few beads assign yourself to a bead by saying, "And I am an expression of Joy."

- Notice how it feels to make this assertion.

- Continue in this manner, moving from one bead to the next with your eyes closed as names arise. Do the practice for at least 10 minutes or a minimum of 20 beads.

- When you feel you have gained sufficient insights, give gratitude for what has been learned, open your eyes, and get on with your day.

The most important part of this exercise is to notice what sensations, thoughts, and feelings arise each time you assert that a certain person is Joy in expression. Your reaction will indicate whether your thoughts and belief systems are aligned with the ego/human aspects of the self or with the more spacious aspects of the Self.

For someone who has no idea that they are the soul temporarily in a human body, it might seem absurd to declare that any human is a direct expression of Source or Joy. If you have come this far in your Earth School journey, you likely understand the concept, even if you haven't yet internalized it as truth.

As you clear away the clouds of human conditioning, you will find it quite natural to see those you love as Joy in expression. This does not mean that you or they are always joyful in human terms. It simply means that you see their inner Light. You recognize them soul to soul.

Where this exercise truly pays off is not when considering those with whom you already resonate. The spiritual "win" comes when the names of people who rub you the wrong way arise. Spirit may play with you and put the names of two politicians from opposing parties next to each other as you work through the beads. Those in the higher realms know exactly how to lovingly push your buttons for the soul's growth.

You will likely hesitate and experience a visceral reaction as you contemplate putting specific people's names and any reference to the Divine in the same sentence.

Do it anyway.

Do it purposefully.

Do not miss this opportunity to push the boundaries of your comfort zone and observe with great interest how your ego rushes to defend your human BS.

The ultimate goal of the Joy-Us Beads Exercise is to remain in soul awareness and move easily from one bead to another without hesitation. If you simply can't accept that certain people could be Joy in expression, now is the time to return to the practice of Questioning What Is. Allow ego to rebel as it will and reread relevant sections of Part I.

Unawakened humans are used to calling names and putting labels on people. This exercise takes name-calling to a w-holy new level.

Observe how your understanding expands as you periodically return to this exercise. Instead of judging others from the human point of view, you will recognize that the soul is within everyone, no matter how obscured.

This does not mean that you approve of hurtful human words and behaviors. You can still take appropriate human action to deal with ignorance. At the same time, the practice produces the compassion that opens the door to solutions that might otherwise never manifest.

Just like our physical bodies, the beads may be different sizes or colors, yet no one bead is any more important than another. There is no hierarchy at the level of the soul. The aspect of you that never changes is the same in every human being. All are Joy in expression.

The more you remove the lens of your conditioned human thinking, the more you will flow effortlessly and Joyously through the bead exercise. To recognize your friends and family members as Joy in expression is a blessing. To recognize that strangers and even those who repel you are also Joy in expression is transformational.

PRACTICE:
OCEAN BREATHING

To sit on a beach and watch the waves wash against the shore is mesmerizing. One after another the swells rise from the vast expanse of water and dissolve in a mass of hissing foam against the shore. It is a never-ending cycle that speaks to the soul.

The magnificence of the ocean with its uninterrupted undulations is familiar to the deeper parts of you. The soul recognizes the eternal patterns of life arising and subsiding within all things. This is Oneness. This is flow.

As this recognition bubbles up from soul awareness to your conscious human experience, what do you do? You pull out your smartphone, put your back to the water, and take a selfie.

You need pictures of special moments like these because the normal human experience is quite different from a day at the beach. Blame the left hemisphere of your brain for the disparity. Unlike the hypnotic flow of ocean waves, the left brain divides existence into blocks of time with finite beginnings and endings. It causes you to label, categorize, and pigeonhole objects and experiences rather than feeling your innate unity.

For an immediate, personal experience of how the left brain operates, glance up from the page and gaze around you. Notice that as your head moves to take in the scene, your eyes come to rest in succession ever so briefly upon the objects in view. What seems like a flowing motion as your head turns is punctuated with almost imperceptible pauses as the brain busily identifies and labels each item.

This is part of the body's built-in survival system. Cavemen stayed alive by paying attention to external objects and assessing potential threats. The oldest part of your brain continues to do the same for you now, even though you and the human brain have evolved since prehistoric times.

The first attendees of Earth School may not have sat around discussing the soul, but even Neanderthals felt and appreciated the grandeur of mountains and the majesty of the sea. This innate appreciation of nature and beauty arises from the soul and thus is present in every human.

Today, increasing numbers of people are becoming aware of their multidimensional nature. They are learning to align with Higher Consciousness by accessing more spacious states. This shift from objective to subjective experience allows modern humans to become reacquainted with their vastness.

Ocean Breathing is a powerful practice designed to reconnect you consciously with your true nature. It bypasses the normal human way of processing visual input and allows you to see and experience the world more as the soul does.

Using the natural rhythms of the breath, you can attune to the flow state of the brain's right hemisphere. This leads to a more balanced and intuitive approach to life throughout your day, even when you're not using Ocean Breathing.

The process is simple, yet it requires a clear intention and a steadfast but relaxed focus. Without these you will easily fall back on the instinctual human mode of seeing, breathing, and being.

Here's how to do it:

- Take one slow, deep breath with the intention of becoming centered. Exhale a bit longer than you inhale to help you relax.

- Inhale slowly again through your nose or your mouth and begin to gaze around you.

- As you exhale, soften your gaze and release your identification with your human role. The body still exists. It is part of the All, but intention allows you to now dissolve into simply being This . . . here . . . now . . . Aware Awareness . . . *being.*

- Experience yourself as the breath and flow outward. Let your gaze wander freely.

- As you encounter objects, you, Awareness, don't stop or go around them; you flow through them.

- When you reach the end of the exhalation, gently flow as the inbreath back to the center, drawing Awareness back into the physical body.

- Continue in this way, maintaining a soft gaze and the fluid movement of Awareness. It may help to visualize an infinity symbol with Awareness flowing out and returning ceaselessly to the center point.

- As your breath goes out in all directions from the center, try repeating thoughts that amplify the reason for doing this exercise, such as "I am one with all that is," "There is no separation as Aware Awareness," or simply state, "Flowing . . ."

Continue breathing in this cyclical manner. Observe Awareness rippling outward like a pebble dropped into the water. As you relax more deeply into this hypnotic, circular flow, you will find yourself merging in awareness with all objects in your path. Trees, birds, and people are no longer separate from you but part of the one experience of Spirit exhaling and inhaling.

Exhaling, you are the omnipresent ocean of Awareness, flowing outward in all directions from one central point. As you inhale, Awareness contracts into one wave. You are not separate from the ocean but arise and dissolve back into the great Sea of Consciousness with the soft sound of breath.

You will naturally experience a heightened state of presence while doing Ocean Breathing. Use this spaciousness to note what fresh, helpful, healing insights arise.

You can do Ocean Breathing anytime, but it is best to practice when you don't need to interact with others for at least five minutes. The length of time you spend doing the exercise is not as important as the quality of your efforts. Ideally you will practice several times a day for five to ten minutes per session.

Work Ocean Breathing into your normal daily activities and practice in various settings. It is especially pleasant to do while walking in nature.

Over time, these periods of practicing conscious unity awareness will gently push out deeply ingrained thoughts of separation from your subconscious mind. The result is a state of harmony with all things and all creatures in your normal waking state. This is the gift of getting to know your true nature: feeling the Loving, Open Wholeness as you FLOW like water through life.

MAINTAINING DAILY ENERGETIC HYGIENE

If you're like most people, you shower or bathe daily. You brush your teeth twice a day, and you wash your hands countless times as needed. You likely have a favorite soap, special lotions, sprays, and gels to make sure your skin, hair, and nails look and smell their best. Most of us attend to this kind of daily physical hygiene routine because we recognize its importance.

The same cannot be said about the attention given to the human energy field.

The vibrational patterns that make up your physical body are part of a dynamic, flowing system. Your human energy field naturally seeks to maintain balance in the physical body, but your human thoughts and behaviors can be at odds with this natural, vibrant flow.

The ongoing interaction of opposites in the earthly dimension subjects your energy field to constantly fluctu-ating frequencies. Many of these are diametrically opposed to the higher vibrations of the soul's natural state. Lower vibrations in the human energy field are equivalent to dirt and grime that build up over time if not cleansed.

Failure to maintain your energetic hygiene can have the same effect as neglecting your physical body's cleanli-ness: it is not healthy, and people may start to avoid you.

The tools in this section are your soap and water. Some are the equivalent of a daily shower. Others are like wash-ing your hands—they are to be used as needed.

At any given moment of the day, your energy field is either in harmony with the Universal Field or in a dishar-monious state. When listening to music, you intuitively know when a singer is off-key. Likewise, your body and mind will tell you when your energy field is out of tune with your true nature.

Discordant emotions and physical pain are the sur-face effects of an underlying energetic imbalance. If you ignore these warning signs, larger blockages may occur. Pain and discomfort, whether emotional or physical, can easily result in disease. You may find that your relation-ships become challenging and your default state is one of irritation or annoyance.

Thankfully, with awareness of your state of being from moment to moment and the use of energy balanc-ing exercises, you can tune your energy field as deftly as a skilled musician.

This section introduces several simple practices that can rapidly bring you to a state of harmony. Far from a placebo and more powerful than any pill, the skills intro-duced here will instantly improve your mood, increase your energy, and provide a positive, new perspective on your earthly challenges.

Even if you are already lucid enough to monitor your thoughts and maintain a peaceful state, you do not live in isolation. You must still interact with other humans who may not be aware of the importance of maintaining a high-vibrational state.

You, at the soul level, know the difference between sharp and flat tones.

Your life may be flowing beautifully when an event or unexpected encounter knocks you off balance. An acquaintance may call to rant about their challenges. You might read an upsetting headline. A rude driver may cut you off on the highway, or you might have a run-in with an angry client. Any number of daily events can have a detrimental effect on your personal energy field.

For this reason, your nonphysical body must be regularly tuned, just like any fine instrument.

This begins with watching what you feed your mind. Turn off the news if you can't watch it without becoming upset. A quick scan of the headlines is all you need to stay on top of current events. Avoid violent entertainment. Choose only friends and social media options that uplift and inspire you. Observe your thoughts and test how they feel in your energetic heart. Pause before you speak. Recognize that not everything requires a response on your part.

The cells in your physical body are doing their best to maintain your health and well-being. They will seek harmony and balance, but you must give them good energy to work with.

You cannot see or measure your human energy field, but it is very real. Try the practices. Feel the immediate positive results. The difference before and after will convince you of the importance of making energetic self-care a priority.

PRACTICE:
VAGUS NERVE BREATHING

You are being breathed by a powerful Force. Try to hold your breath. You will be successful for a short period until the survival mechanisms of the body take over. This is far from a mechanistic response. It is the result of Love in Full Expression flowing through you.

The Life Force greets your earthly experience with your first inhalation and departs your physical body with the final exhalation. It moves with the breath in cyclical patterns that mimic the larger dynamics of creation. Each incarnation is one breath in the life cycles of the soul.

Most people pay far too little attention to the breath. They are unaware that as a purveyor of Presence, the breath holds the key to increased vitality and emotional well-being. When you are stressed, breathing becomes rapid and shallow. This is the opposite of the type of breathing you need most when under pressure.

Thankfully, your body is created with systems that help to regulate your breathing. They are perfectly designed to deal with the inevitable stressors of Earth School:

- The sympathetic nervous system is in charge of the "fight or flight" syndrome. This response kicks in whenever your body senses danger, whether real or perceived, physical or emotional. Your heart rate, breathing, and blood pressure increase. Adrenaline and cortisol rush through your body.

- The parasympathetic nervous system does the opposite. Known as the "rest and digest" system, it helps your body to relax when under stress.

Vagus Nerve Breathing, sometimes called vagal breathing, is a conscious practice that allows you to capitalize on the parasympathetic nervous system's benefits.

The vagus is the longest nerve in the autonomic nervous system. It runs from the base of your brain through your neck and chest to your abdomen. When you put pressure on the vagus nerve with your rib cage through a special type of deep breathing, this action triggers your body's relaxation response. The result is instant physical and mental relief. (Can you say, "Ahhhhhh"?)

Many spiritual practices encourage "belly breathing," where you focus on expanding the abdomen as you inhale. This is an excellent, healthy way to breathe anytime to increase the flow of oxygen and Life Force throughout your body. It is not the same as vagal breathing.

When you expand your abdomen with breath, you may not exert enough pressure on the vagus nerve to induce relaxation. In vagal breathing you add a few extra seconds of mild but deliberate exertion to normal belly breathing.

To practice vagal breathing:

- Set the intention that your efforts will relax your mind and body.

- Take in a slow, deep breath through the nose.

- Using your abdominal muscles, push your belly outward as you inhale to fill your lungs completely.

- Count off the seconds as you inhale. To ensure you are breathing slowly enough, the first few times you practice vagal breathing, you may want to silently state, "One thousand one, one thousand two, one thousand three," and so forth. An inhalation of four to five seconds is sufficient to fill your lungs.

- When you reach the apex of the inhalation, begin the outbreath without pausing.

- Count off the seconds as you exhale through slightly pursed lips. The goal is to exhale longer than you inhaled. During the last few extra seconds, use mild effort to expel every bit of air from your lungs.

- Pay attention to the sensation that occurs in this final push. Your chest and rib cage should contract noticeably. This is the crucial point where you are putting pressure on the vagus nerve.

During normal inhalations and exhalations, the physical sensations of breathing are so commonplace that you aren't usually aware of them. With vagal breathing you *want* to notice a strong contraction.

In response to this pressure, signals travel immediately to the brain. Your heart rate slows, your blood pressure drops, and you reap the reward of instant serenity.

Pause now to take a few vagal breaths. Before you begin, assess your current state of "peace versus tension." Assess this again after only one breath. Repeat as necessary until you register a noticeable improvement.

This natural practice puts the power of maintaining your energetic and physical health under your conscious control. Try vagal breathing the next time you have your blood pressure taken. As you breathe with the cuff on your arm, hold the intention that your blood pressure will settle at the optimal level. Be prepared to explain your secret when the practitioner compliments you on an improvement from your normal reading.

Your body naturally seeks peace. You see evidence of this in the act of sighing. With awareness, you can consciously harness the power of the breath and breathe a sigh of relief.

Once you personally experience the dramatic effects of Vagus Nerve Breathing, you will want to do it often. Use it to get grounded when the extremes of being human knock you off balance. One vagal breath will stop a craving in its tracks by instantly relieving the stress that causes you to want to overindulge. Try Vagus Nerve Breathing when you notice you are about to say or do something that is out of alignment with your true nature.

Vagal breathing helps you find the middle ground. It is no accident that the heart, lungs, and the powerful vagus nerve converge at the center of your physical body. When you focus awareness on the core of your being and become present with the breath, you will come to know what it means to be centered.

PRACTICE:
THE CROSSBAR TECHNIQUE

As anyone who has ever played in the surf knows, it's no fun to be tossed about in big waves. Living in a human body is like floating on a raft. You try to keep your balance, but you're at the mercy of the local conditions.

The sensations, thoughts, and feelings that arise from the Sea of Consciousness cause energetic effects much like ocean waves. The ups and downs inherent in the human experience can toss the raft out from under you when you least expect it.

The Crossbar Technique is a quick and easy tool that brings you back into alignment with your Higher Self. It combines mental visualization with a simple movement of your arms to help you regain stability.

The technique is based on the understanding that the experiences of every being in all possible realities arise within one shared Mind. It requires you to acknowledge that you—a soul playing a human role—are a direct projection of the sensations, thoughts, and feelings of this one indivisible Mind. You are indivisibly connected with the Source of energy that enlivens you.

As a soul, you have the choice at any time to get caught up in the projection or to step back mentally and observe what is being projected. Shifting from the Experiencer to the Observer will always put you in a place of power.

Anytime you realize that you are out of sorts or uncentered, use this awareness to remind yourself that you are a soul playing out your human role. In this moment of clarity, shift to the soul's point of view and do the Cross-bar Technique as follows:

- Stand straight, tall, and relaxed.

- Breathe slowly and deeply as you step back in awareness from your human role.

- Review with detached curiosity the elements of your story that have brought you to an unbalanced state.

- Affirm that you are part of a dynamic, interactive flow of energies that relate to the various states of being.

- Visualize a vertical flow of energy that runs from high above your head and grounds you into the earth. This is the axis that energetically connects you, the soul, with the Universal Field or One Mind.

- Acknowledge and move your attention to an equivalent horizontal energy axis running from one side of you to the other at chest level. This bar represents your earthly, human focus.

- Assess how far off center you felt before you began this exercise. Physically place your hands on the imaginary horizontal bar at a point representative of your current state. For example, if you are at your wit's end, you would place your hands out as far to each side as you can reach. If you are mildly unbalanced, you would grasp the horizontal axis with your hands close in and elbows touching your sides. You should be holding your hands and arms out as if ready to bench press a heavy bar from a standing position.

- With the intention of bringing the horizontal/human axis into alignment with the vertical/soul axis, begin to slowly twist the crossbar around the pivot point at the heart. Physically make this motion, taking approximately four to five seconds to complete the turn. The first few times you do this practice, you may want to silently count, "One thousand one, one thousand two, one thousand three," and so forth to get a sense for how slowly to rotate the bar.

  o Note: Kinesthetically it is easier to perform this twisting motion if one fist faces up and the other down. Twist in the direction your fists are facing.

- When your hands come into alignment with your head and torso, one will be somewhere around the head and the other will be somewhere around your pubic bone, depending on how far out of balance you were when you began. At this wonderful point of alignment, open your fists and spread your fingers wide. You may sense the upward energetic release that occurs.

- Visualize all unwanted, story-based energy being swept up the vertical axis and removed completely from your energy field.

o   Note how it feels to once again be
    centered and aligned. Shake out
    your hands and send a wave of
    gratitude to the Universe for this
    energetic upgrade.

You are a multidimensional being. There is a distinct, dynamic flow associated with each level of your existence, and each is intimately interconnected. The Crossbar Technique asks you to visualize energetic currents that are very real.

Pay attention as you shift from the scattered human energies to the more stable flow of the soul's energy field. The more these fields come into alignment, the more you will experience the steady state of your deepest essence.

PRACTICE:
CHAKRA BALANCING

———

Vagus Nerve Breathing and the Crossbar Technique are the "hand washing" of energy work. Like cleaning your hands, they are helpful to practice multiple times throughout the day and are especially useful when you need a quick dust-off.

When it comes to energetic hygiene, chakra balancing is the shower. You could go a day or two without it, but it is best done daily.

Chakras are the major energy exchange points between your physical and etheric bodies. They act much like a valve, facilitating the flow of the Life Force to and through you. Your body and mind are powered by this Life Force energy, which is also known as prana, chi, or ki. The chakras act like traffic circles, routing the flow from the greater field to your physical organs and systems in the immediate area of each energy center as needed. The "traffic" is made up of the sensations, thoughts, and feelings traveling through your personal field of awareness in ever-changing patterns and frequencies.

While the soul enlivens the body, prana never stops moving completely, but lower-frequency ST-F can easily cause a slowdown or even a backup in the flow. Energetic blockages manifest in a variety of ways at the physical level, including bad moods, lethargy, and general malaise. Over time, these sluggish areas can turn emotional disease into actual physical illness or can result in an emotional state of constant irritation or annoyance.

When balancing the chakras, most people tend to focus on energetic blockages, but the flow of energy can also be too high. This situation occurs when higher-frequency energy than normal is flowing through your system for extended periods of time.

This might happen when you speak or perform before a group of people. It also occurs when you are exposed to high-vibration events such as a live concert or an exciting movie. If you don't take steps to restore the optimum flow of energy through your chakras when the excitement is over, you might experience insomnia, headaches, dizziness, or even nausea.

ST-F happens. You can't always control your initial responses to the moment by moment events in your life. You have even less control over other people's thoughts, words, and actions. As an energetic being, you are directly affected by these constantly changing conditions. Happily, just as you can take a shower when your physical body gets a bit dirty, you can cleanse your energetic body when it needs to be refreshed.

I received an e-mail from a physicist who had been working with a massage therapist to relieve stress. She recommended that he work with his chakras as part of a program of self-care. He told me that he had found plenty of information online about the subject, but he found nothing convincing. He wanted my opinion about whether chakras are real.

I replied that he could do all the research he wanted, but he wouldn't find scientific proof of the existence of chakras. Humans have not yet developed scientific instruments sensitive enough to detect these energetic vortices that vibrate at a frequency beyond our measurable electromagnetic spectrum. I recommended that he engage in a bit of self-science and do the chakra balancing practice I will share with you in this section. If he felt better afterward, that was all the proof he needed.

Energy flows where your attention goes. When you hold the intention that each energy center will find the perfect state of flow, the chakras will do the rest. The innate intelligence of the body works with you to find its own center.

This means that you don't have to be sensitive enough to notice whether your chakras are blocked or overexpanded, nor do you have to note exactly where the imbalance is. You can focus on each chakra in succession or on all of them at once. Both methods work. Simply set the intention that all your chakras come into perfect balance and alignment.

Just like a shower with soap and water, the length of the practice depends on how much cleaning you need. Here is how you might balance your chakras if you are feeling noticeably disconnected and out of sorts:

- Sit or lie quietly where you won't be disturbed for about ten minutes. You may find it helpful to listen to relaxing meditation music as you do the practice.

- Assess your current state of well-being. Rate how you feel mentally, physically, and emotionally.

- Take a few breaths to relax and become centered.

- Imagine a shaft of white light flowing from above your head and going down, around, and through you, anchoring you into the earth.

- Visualize seven glowing spheres of energy aligned vertically along this central channel inside your body. The accepted names, location, and colors as described by those who can psychically see and sense the body's energy fields are:

  o The first/root/base chakra is located at the base of the spine and is associated with the color red.

  o The second/sacral chakra is in the center of the abdomen and is associated with the color orange.

  o The third/solar plexus chakra is located at the level of the navel and is associated with the color yellow.

  o The fourth/heart chakra is at the level of the heart and is associated with the color emerald green.

  o The fifth/throat chakra is in the center of the throat and is associated with a baby blue color.

  o The sixth/third eye chakra is located in the center of the skull at the level of the eyebrows and is associated with the color indigo.

  o The seventh/crown chakra sits atop the skull, outside the body, and is associated with the color violet.

- Move your awareness to the first chakra and picture its associated color. Visualize Life Force energy flowing perfectly into, around, and through this center. Spend as much time as you feel guided to focusing on perfect balance and alignment before moving your awareness upward to the next chakra.

- Repeat this process as you move through each subsequent chakra in turn, allowing yourself to be guided as to how much time to spend on each one and what imagery you might use to visualize them coming into balance.

- When you have focused on all seven chakras and used intention and visualization to help each find its perfect flow state, trust that healing has taken place.

- Assess how you feel at the end of the exercise compared to how you felt before you began.

- Send a wave of gratitude to the Universe for your renewed well-being.

The effects of a thorough chakra balancing like this one will stay with you for several hours or several days. Just like cleaning your physical body, however, dust and dirt accumulate through daily living. It is vitally important to your energetic health and your ability to connect with higher realms that you balance your chakras regularly and when something particularly upsetting happens to you.

If you are maintaining your energetic health and want a quick inner "rinse," you can choose to do an abbreviated chakra balancing practice. Here are two quick and easy methods that work well to refresh and recharge:

1. Whether standing or sitting, close your eyes and visualize a wall of shimmering golden light in front of you. Using intention and imagination, see the wall moving slowly toward you and passing through you. As it does so, the fine mesh of this golden wall picks up any energetic "dust and dirt" that doesn't belong in your field. Visualize the wall moving away behind you, carrying off what is no longer needed.

   To be sure your field is as clean and sparkly as possible. You can move the wall back in the opposite direction, passing from behind you to the front, picking up any stray energetic "debris" that might have been missed on the first pass through.

   I jokingly call this the Car Wash Method of chakra balancing. Try it. It works.

2. Visualize a shaft of white light moving up within the larger shaft of light that grounds you into the earth. This smaller shaft swirls around you in a clockwise motion, starting at the feet and moving upward.

   As this rotating light passes around and through each of the seven chakras, hold the intention that it balances each in turn. You may find it helpful to move your hand in a spiral motion up the front of your body and release any unwanted energy with a flourish when you reach the crown.

   I call this the Roto-Rooter Method of Chakra Clearing. (Humor is great for lifting your vibration.)

Adopt a state of childlike curiosity when doing these exercises. As I told the skeptical physicist, the proof is in the results. Personal experience will show you that balancing your chakras is more effective and fast-acting than any mood-enhancing, energy-lifting drug when you are feeling out of balance.

Life in human form is challenging. You have to contend with not only your own shifting thoughts and emotions but also those of others. It's no wonder most people aren't aware of the higher dimensions. They are so mired in the energetic traffic jams of daily living that they can't find their way to the alternate destinations.

Chakra clearing puts you back in the driver's seat with a range of routes to take for optional functioning.

PRACTICE:
CLEARING PHYSICAL SPACES

Have you ever entered a room and felt your skin crawl for no apparent reason? You were likely picking up the energy in the space.

Everything in physical existence has an energetic signature. People, places, and things are patterns of vibration with unique frequencies. Each object or thought form leaves an imprint in the space in which it vibrates. Patterns that are repeated over time in the same contained space have a cumulative effect that can be sensed in conscious awareness.

Examples of places where even those who don't consider themselves sensitive might notice the unique energy include:

- Churches, temples, or synagogues
- Meditation rooms
- Hospitals
- Prisons
- Battlefields

As you review this list, you can imagine the kind of energy each would carry. Know that such sensations would not be imaginary if you were to step into these places. Your human energy field would merge with the energy fields present, and information would then arise in Awareness as sensations, thoughts, and feelings. The more sensitive you are, the more details you could discern from this ST-F, ranging from basic emotions to facts about specific events that occurred there.

Understanding that energy can remain in a space long after an event occurred can explain why you might experience inappropriate emotions and moods that have no apparent cause. Remember: not every thought or feeling is your own.

As an example, my husband and I once received a dinner invitation to the home of new friends in our community. We followed directions to their house and, to our surprise, discovered they had bought the home of another couple we used to socialize with. We had attended several parties in the house and knew it well.

When our new friends greeted us at the door, we told them about our familiarity with their home. I revealed that the previous owners had gone through a very nasty divorce, which is why they sold the house.

The couple shared a look of surprise followed by dawning comprehension. They informed us that they normally got along very well, but they had inexplicably been at each other's throats for the first month in their new house. They had attributed the bickering to the stress of moving, yet they had moved several times before with no such problems.

With this new information, they understood that there was nothing wrong in their relationship. They had simply picked up the lingering negative energy from the previous owners' interactions. It had taken a month for their positive, loving energy to override the stale, lower energy left in the house.

Had they known about the effects of fields and understood that it's possible to clear and refresh the energy in a space, they could have avoided unnecessary angst.

I learned this important lesson about stagnant energy when I started doing readings for clients. As a new medium, I noticed that after working with about six hundred clients, the clarity of my connections across the veil began to decline. I often rate the connection by comparing it to a cell phone signal. The goal is always to have a "five-bar" connection.

I became concerned when over a period of two weeks I experienced several three-bar sessions. This was unacceptable, so I went into meditation and asked my guides what was going on.

You have worked with many clients in this room, my main guide replied, *and you have never cleared the energy.*

I was stunned. No one had ever told me I needed to do such a thing. The more I thought about it, the more it made sense. Most of my clients were dealing with deep grief or were experiencing emotional pain from trauma. I could see how the accumulated energy of so many people could adversely affect my workspace.

My guide instructed me to learn all I could about clearing energetic spaces. He warned me that rituals are helpful, but the most important element in any practice is intention.

I had heard of people using sage, but I had dismissed it as a New Age practice with no basis in "reality." Trusting fully in my guides, I researched various ways to clear energy in physical spaces. To my surprise, I learned that the use of sage is not new at all. Various cultures throughout history have benefited from the cleansing properties of this natural plant.

Other plants such as palo santo and cedar work well for clearing energy, but the energetic frequency of sage is particularly suited for this purpose. Indigenous peoples have very specific processes surrounding the cultivation, care, and use of what is considered a sacred plant. To honor these beliefs and practices is to tap into the power of the group consciousness surrounding them.

The vibration of specific sounds can also remove unwanted energy and refresh a space quite effectively. Examples include ringing bells and clapping your hands as you walk throughout the room or facility and envision all lower vibrations dissolving. You may also experiment with the use of lighted candles and certain stones known for their energy clearing properties.

Having done my research and consulted with my guides, I gathered the materials that resonated with my own beliefs. I moved about the room where I do my readings and affirmed that my actions were clearing out all but the most beneficial energy.

Was it my imagination that the room felt fresh and clear after my ceremony? Not at all. I enjoyed a marked improvement in clarity in the readings that followed. The five-bar signal returned.

Since then, I clear the energy and my own field regularly. I strongly recommend you do so:

- When moving into a new house

- When staying in hotel rooms (It's not just the strange bed that causes you to sleep poorly when traveling. You are subconsciously sensing the unfamiliar energy of previous guests long after they've departed.)

- When leading groups in public places
- When there has been an unpleasant interaction in a particular room
- When someone who is not well has stayed in a room
- In your workspace
- In hospital rooms
- Anywhere else you can think of that doesn't feel uplifting

Maintain a strong intention as you conduct your clearing rituals. In doing so, you will witness the Law of Conservation of Energy in action. It states that energy cannot be created or destroyed, merely transformed. This awareness provides the key to living peacefully amid fluctuating fields. The positive difference you notice before and after clearing the energy will convince you of the benefits.

INTERACTING WITH HIGHER CONSCIOUSNESS

You are *This, Here, Now . . . Aware Awareness* expressing itself as you, a soul. You, the soul, are expressing yourself in human form for the experience of it. What a Joy it is to be aware of This and live in This-Awareness!

Why aren't most people aware they are magnificent multidimensional beings while in human form? Because they spend their time focused on the outer world. Rather than humans *being*, they are humans *doing*.

Sound familiar?

Most likely, from the moment you awaken in the morning, your mental activity rarely slows down. The focus of your attention jumps from one sensation, thought, and feeling to the next. The Buddhist term *monkey mind* refers to this tendency of human minds to be fidgety and curious.

The ego turns this restlessness into multitasking, which is great for getting a lot done in human terms. Unfortunately, all that *doing* keeps you from being still and knowing I AM.

The spaciousness of the soul is always accessible, but its presence is eclipsed by the attractions of the external world. *The Story of Me* is far more interesting to the ego than silence. Without a concerted effort to bypass the ego and hit the mental Pause switch on a regular basis, you can easily forget that this world is not the only reality. The inevitable result of this lack of expanded awareness is stress.

Peace is but one breath away. Always. You cannot be separated from the spaciousness of the soul. You are always connected to Higher Consciousness. With intention, you can deliberately remove your focus from the content of your story and align with the soul. From this expanded state, you can shift to any other "channel" within the One Universal Network.

Which nonphysical beings would it be helpful to interact with? Would you like to feel the presence of a family member who has passed and enjoy a conversation with them? Were there things left unsaid when your loved one left this world? Would you like to provide or receive explanations for events in your life? Is there advice you would ask for from your spirit guides? Do you have a question for an archangel or a mythological figure?

Each of these connections and more are well within your ability as a soul. Because all beings arise from the same Source, you are fully capable of interacting with whomever you desire. Those in the higher realms are ready to help you fulfill your purpose here in Earth School if your requests serve the greater good. They will respond to your efforts and prove their presence in magical ways when your intentions come from the heart.

Belief, intention, and attention are the three keys to making the connection with Higher Consciousness. First, believe that your normal waking state of consciousness is one of limitless states that you can access. Second, set and hold the clear intention to access these higher states as needed for assistance, comfort, and healing. Third, focus and hold your attention beyond your story while exploring other realms.

This section introduces you to proven practices to do precisely that. You will learn here to quiet the monkey mind and explore your expansive nature. I want to issue a strong advisory, however, to not necessarily expect knock-your-socks-off experiences each time you enter your inner world. This can set you up for disappointment.

Remember, you are always already connected with Higher Consciousness. What you are seeking is awareness of this truth. The key, as I learned in my efforts to connect with my stepdaughter, Susan, is persistence and consistency in your efforts.

Please understand as you hold the intention of connecting with Higher Consciousness that even the moments when nothing seems to be happening are valuable. Every moment you spend sitting in the silence allows you to focus on the clear sky while the inevitable clouds of ordinary ST-F bubble up in awareness. It is then—as the clouds fade into the background—that you come face to face with your fundamental nature as Awareness, itself.

Do the practices in this section with an open mind and the playfulness and curiosity of a child. Make the commitment to continue until you achieve your intention. Your efforts will be rewarded in coming to know yourself as something far greater than the limited human self.

As long as you are in a body, your brain will filter out awareness of the higher dimensions. The methods that follow will train you how to temporarily bypass that filter. You will learn how to dissolve into your heart space and engage with loving beings who are right here, right now. Whether you do so for moments or minutes, the experiences will change you.

Once you regularly access the part of you that never changes, you will more easily notice the contrast between human nature and your true nature. Over time, you will gravitate toward the latter and make more harmonious choices from moment to moment.

It is no small thing to discover how very special you are and how cherished. When you shift back to your human role, you will take This Awareness with you. You will no longer need your story or the people in it to conform to your desires to know true happiness.

THE BLESS ME METHOD

SEVEN STEPS TO CONNECTING WITH HIGHER CONSCIOUSNESS

Connecting with beings in the various nonphysical realms is easy and natural for the soul. It does not require traveling in a geographical sense, for all realities interpenetrate one another.

To better understand the omnipresence of all realities, think in terms of television signals. The various frequencies of hundreds of channels are all around you, but the brain is not tuned to their bandwidth. You need a special receiver to detect these signals.

The process of watching a movie on TV is stunningly similar to the steps you can use to connect with beings in the nonphysical realms. If you analyze what actually occurs beneath your conscious awareness when you entertain the thought of watching a show, you will discover that you go through several steps to do so:

- You set the intention to watch a movie.

- You research what movies are playing.

- You choose a movie, noting the channel and time.

- At the intended time, you turn on the television.

- You focus your attention on the screen.

- Using the remote control, you shift to the correct channel.

- You watch the program and enjoy the ST-F (sensations, thoughts, and feelings) that arise with the experience.

- If you don't resonate with the movie, you can change the channel at any time without going anywhere. You simply press the button on the remote control for a different experience.

It's simple. It's natural.

And so it is with adventures in consciousness. You normally don't sense different realities due to the brain's filtering mechanism, but all dimensions are right *here*, right now in awareness.

The tendency while in a human body is to stay tuned only to the Earth School channel. This is a very narrow slice of the total bandwidth available to you. While it's true that you are here for the full human experience, you are limiting yourself by not exploring your many options.

As a soul, you have access to the Universal Studio, the source of all available channels. By properly attuning your human energy field, the ST-F of different realities can appear on your screen of Awareness.

Just like the example above of watching a movie on TV, you don't really need to think through the process of attuning to Higher Consciousness. Once you understand what's going on at both the subconscious and conscious level, you can "change the channel" at will.

There are people who enjoy a personal relationship with angels and guides with no effort. Some have seen or sensed discarnate beings since childhood. If you were to ask them how they connect and interact with higher-frequency beings, they would likely shrug their shoulders and reply, "I just do it!"

When I first started teaching others to connect with those in the nonphysical realms, I knew I would have many students who would want to know the precise "how-tos" of connecting across the veil. Telling them "you just do it" wouldn't cut it. Such an approach certainly wouldn't have worked for me when I was still relying more on the left hemisphere of my brain for navigating reality.

I pondered the varied situations through which I interacted with those in the spirit world and how I did so. I realized that I follow the same process each time to go from normal waking consciousness to the optimal state in which to experience and engage with beings in other dimensions.

I broke the procedure down into the specific actions that produce the desired results. With just a little tweaking for the sake of making it easy to remember, I delineated seven steps that flow naturally from one to the next: breathe, lift, expand, surrender/set aside, shift, merge, and experience/engage. These form the acronym "BLESS ME."

I have since taught this method to tens of thousands of students. It is logical and systematic, taking you through the seven steps in three stages: preparatory, transitional, and experiential. Focusing on each letter as you go through the steps keeps the mind from wandering.

For this reason, The BLESS ME Method is especially helpful for those who tend to favor the left hemisphere of the brain. Some of the steps involve only one action, and you perform them the same each time. Others allow you to pick and choose which activities you will do to complete the stage. This brings in the right hemisphere to balance things out as you flow from one stage to the next. The built-in flexibility ensures a fresh experience each time so that the process is never rote or rigid.

The process works because it helps you achieve a deeper state of expanded awareness more quickly and easily than other less structured methods. Seasoned meditators have found it so useful that they have modified decades of practice to incorporate The BLESS ME Method into their regular practice.

With the overarching goal of attuning to Higher Consciousness, you can use The BLESS ME Method as I do for a variety of intentions, such as:

- To commune and communicate with guides, angels, and loved ones who have passed, either your own or those of others

- To access guidance and insights for dealing with your earthly challenges

- To explore other dimensions of reality

- To train your mind to be still

- To sit in awareness of your limitless nature

- To experience the peace of simply being

You should plan to do the practice when you have at least ten minutes of uninterrupted time. Once you begin, you will stay in each stage until you intuitively know it's time to move on to the next one. The BLESS ME Method can be considered meditation, but it is both an active and a passive mental activity depending on which stage you are in.

The specific instructions for the practice follow. It's actually a very easy process that I summarize in a simple list after the details. I go into depth here first so that you understand the purpose of each step as well as how to perform them.

I have also provided a sample meditation at the end of the description to model how the steps beautifully flow together.

BEFORE YOU BEGIN

Always have a clear intention, even if it is simply to sit in the silence and see what unfolds. Other possible intentions are listed in the previous section.

Choose a quiet place where you won't be disturbed. Sit or lie comfortably with your eyes closed. You may find it helpful to visualize yourself surrounded by a shaft of white light to sense your interconnection with the upper realms and the earth.

STEP 1: BREATHE

The purpose of this stage is to slow down your busy mind and relax your body. To that end, note how you feel as you begin the process. You might rate your stress or energy level on a scale of 1 to 10, with a higher number indicating higher stress. Move on only when your rating improves noticeably.

Take in a deep belly breath, inhaling very slowly to the count of four. Exhale to the count of six. The extra two seconds on the exhalation are critical. By the count of four, your lungs should be nearly empty if you are inhaling and exhaling at the same rate. On counts five and six, you will have to exert extra pressure to continue blowing out air. In doing so, your diaphragm cage will press against the vagus nerve that runs along your spine. As you learned in Section 2, pressure on the vagus nerve triggers the body's relaxation response. For this practice, you want your body to be as relaxed as possible.

Take a second vagus breath. As you exhale, mentally scan your body for any tension. Release all tightness you find.

Take a third vagus breath. As you do so, give yourself self-hypnotic suggestions to help you relax as fully as possible. For example, *I am sinking deeper, deeper, deeper into my chair.* Now and then you may want to change the words you use so that the practice doesn't become rote.

After the initial three breaths, your body should be noticeably more relaxed than when you began. Your mind should be peaceful yet alert. If not, continue focusing on your deep breathing. If you are thoroughly relaxed and your mind has noticeably slowed down, move on to the second step. Hold the intention that your breathing remain slow and steady with no more need to focus on it.

STEP 2: LIFT

Your intention in this step is to turn up your inner light. You want to break out of the limited bandwidth of the human energy field to make the higher-frequency realms more accessible. You do this by lifting your frequency using a variety of uplifting techniques until you sense a positive "lift" in how you feel.

Choose activities that allow you to keep your eyes closed and to remain seated or lying down. There are many ways you can engender positive vibrations. For example, you might:

- Bring to mind several things for which you are grateful. (Do it now and feel the shift in your heart area.) Feelings of appreciation, care, and compassion have the same mood-lifting effect.

- Contemplate someone or something that brings you great joy. Feel the Lift in your heart that comes as you focus on these joyous thoughts or experiences.

- Move your awareness to the existential light at the center of you. Visualize it growing increasingly brighter and warmer until your aura—the manifestation of your human energy field—is filled with an intensely bright glow. Imagine those in the nonphysical dimensions being able to see you better as you turn up this light.

- Visualize a favorite place in nature. Completely immerse yourself in the experience of seeing the sights, hearing the sounds, smelling the scents, and feeling sensations on your skin. Experience the joy of being here. (Note that this practice awakens and prepares your soul senses for the final steps in the practice.)

- Silently repeat uplifting affirmations, such as "I AM Love in Full Expression" or "I am so very loved."

- Tone or hum sacred sounds such as "Om."

- Smile.

- Balance your chakras (review the detailed instructions for this practice in the section on energetic hygiene). Do a full extended version if you are feeling particularly out of sorts. Do a quick clearing if you feel only mildly off balance.

Use these techniques in any order, in any combination, one after another. It helps to note how you feel as you begin. Are you out of sorts, feeling a bit low, grumpy, or otherwise not yourself? If so, use every vibration-raising tool in the list above and add a few of your own.

Just as with the first step, "Breathe," remain in this step until you experience a noticeable energetic or emotional Lift. If you begin The BLESS ME Method and you are already feeling vibrant and clear, affirm your gratitude for LIFE and move on.

STEP 3: EXPAND

This step is short, and unlike the very changeable Lift step, you do this one the same way each time. The goal is to expand your focus from your physical body to your vast interconnectedness at the energetic level with all that exists.

Begin by visualizing your aura in a spherical shape around your body. Get a sense for how far out from your body it radiates. Perhaps you imagine it ending a few feet or a few yards from your center.

Using the breath as a vehicle for this mental expansion, inhale through the nose enough to fill your lungs with air. Silently state "Expand" as you exhale through rounded lips, as if trying to blow out a large number of candles on a birthday cake. If done properly, you will produce a sound like a strong wind blowing in the trees.

As you exhale, visualize the boundaries of your aura moving outward in all directions. Your awareness moves with your energy field, expanding with the breath to fill all space.

You may choose to affirm the spacious state you now experience with a phrase such as, "I am limitless!"

This completes the three steps that form the preparatory stages of The BLESS ME Method. Flow seamlessly now to the two steps of the transitional stage. Just like the Expand step, the Surrender/Set Aside and Shift steps are brief, consisting of just a few words, and you perform them the same way each time.

STEP 4: SURRENDER/SET ASIDE

Having relaxed your mind and body and expanded your energy field, the goal of this stage is to release your identification with only your human story. You acknowledge that ego likes to keep you from knowing you are so much more than your physical body and mind. In awareness that you will always have a story as long as you are in a body, you suspend your sole identification with the contents of that story by silently stating, "I surrender."

If the term *surrender* causes you any angst, you may also state "setting aside" as a means of acknowledging that you are temporarily removing your focus from the ego.

STEP 5: SHIFT

Bring to mind the reality you wish to experience and the beings you wish to communicate with, such as the angelic realm, your guides, or the immediate afterlife where loved ones who have passed exist. You may also simply remain open to accessing whatever experience and dimension serves the greatest good.

Using the metaphor of a remote control, energetically "change the channel" by silently stating, "Shift!" The intention behind this word, no matter what reality you wish to access, is to shift from the limited perspective of your human nature to the spacious awareness of the soul.

You may choose to roll your eyes upward without opening them as you say, "Shift!" This motion triggers alpha waves in the brain. Alpha is the optimal brain wave state for spacious awareness. Pause and try this now. See if you notice a pleasant sensation like an elevator lifting. Be sure to allow your eyes to return naturally to their normal closed position. Do not force them to remain looking upward.

Trust that just as pressing the button on a remote control brings about the desired result of changing channels, by clearly stating "Shift!" you have achieved your intention and shifted dimensions. You are now ready to flow seamlessly to the two final steps of The BLESS ME Method that constitute the experiential stage.

STEP 6: MERGE

With the intention to mentally *merge* and connect with a specific higher-frequency being, silently issue them an invitation such as, "Come now."

When you focus your attention on specific higher beings and issue an invitation like this, they energetically pick up on you singling them out. Do so with confidence. You are not bothering them by asking for assistance, no matter what kind of pedestal humans may have placed them on. They hold you in the same esteem you may have for them. They want to help you. Worthiness is a human concept that holds no meaning in the spirit realms. All are loved. All are valued.

Understand that nonphysical beings do not have to move in a physical sense for your fields of awareness to *merge*. At the deeper levels, you are already connected. Saying "Come now" or inviting another being to "Step in close" is a concession to the human way of interacting. You are simply merging with each other in awareness.

Having issued your invitation, trust that it was received. If it serves the greater good and you are properly attuned from doing the previous steps, you are now ready for the final step of The BLESS ME Method.

STEP 7: EXPERIENCE AND ENGAGE

This step is where you fulfill your initial overall intention for the session. Whoever you hoped to engage and whatever you intended to learn or experience will hopefully arise in awareness. Your task is to remain focused and *experience* what ST-F bubbles up. In other words, sit as the blue sky of Awareness and observe the clouds that float by.

The passive aspect of the Experience step makes it an excellent opportunity to practice being present and focus on only one thing: the passing weather. Because you have issued an invitation, you expect ST-F to appear in the sky other than the ordinary clouds of daily human existence.

And so, you sit. And you wait. And you watch with great interest, scanning your entire field of awareness like a radar. What do you sense? What thoughts do you hear? What images do you see?

You may notice ordinary thoughts bubble up as your mind wanders. Let those familiar clouds float by without judgment. Immediately bring your attention back to watching for experiences that match your intention.

Nonphysical beings will use any combination of your nonphysical senses to interact with you. Images may pop into your mind, put there by the beings you hope to communicate with. You may hear words or sense full thoughts that are clearly not your own. You may experience unexpected sensations in your body such as tingling or pressure. You may sense a presence much like you do when someone physically steps into the room.

At the first indication of ST-F that is not what you would identify as "your own" sensations, thoughts, feelings, or images, trust that what you are sensing is coming from a higher being. It stands out in your awareness for a reason!

You can continue to remain passive and simply observe what unfolds or you may now actively *engage* this presence.

If you choose the latter, mentally greet whoever you sense. Inquire who they are if this is not clear and ask any other questions that come to mind. It's critical to sit quietly between each question. Clear your mind repeatedly and return to observing what you *experience*.

If at any time you feel you have dropped the connection, go back to an earlier stage in the process. You may need to Expand or Shift again to reengage. If you ask questions during the Experience stage and don't sense a response, relax. Trust that the answers will come later. They may arrive in ways you don't expect.

Understand that you are not a failure if you don't hear sounds, see lights, or sense the presence of higher beings each time you meditate. Be aware of the human tendency to have expectations for the outcome. This can lead to frustration. You are a unique soul whose human experience is unfolding perfectly for you. You may sense a connection immediately, or it may take a while. You won't know until you give it your best effort.

Remain in the Experience and Engage stage until you sense the session has come to a natural conclusion. You will intuitively know when it is time to return to normal waking consciousness.

Send a wave of gratitude from your heart to the Universe for what has been received and open your eyes.

* * *

Here is The BLESS ME Method in concise form:

- Set a clear intention for your session.

- Take three vagus breaths to become centered and relaxed.

- Use as many mental techniques as necessary to experience a Lift in your vibration.

- State the word *expand* as you send your energy field outward with the breath.

- Surrender/set aside your focus on the ego by stating, "I surrender."

- Move your attention to a different dimension by stating, "Shift!"

- Invite helpful, loving beings to merge their awareness with yours by stating, "Come now."

- Experience what arises in awareness. Engage any sensations, thoughts, and feelings that match your stated intention for this session.

- With gratitude for what has been received, return instantly to normal waking consciousness.

The more you use The BLESS ME Method, the more easily you will flow through the seven steps. In time, you will find your intuition is coming back online after years of relying on the external world for information. You will start to simply "know" things that come to you without using your physical senses. You will notice that you are experiencing more peace throughout your day, reacting in a more positive light to things that used to stress you.

Each time you sit quietly and dedicate yourself to focusing on the silence pays off in ways you may not initially

sense. If you don't have any unusual experiences while practicing The BLESS ME Method, you are not "doing it wrong"
or wasting your time. You are fine-tuning your awareness.

Treat yourself with the same loving patience those in
the higher realms have for you. Stay with the practice. You
will look back someday and see how far you've come.

* * *

For illustrative purposes, what follows is one example
of the limitless ways The BLESS ME Method can unfold.
For this session, the intention is to connect with a guide.
Notice how each step logically and seamlessly flows, one
after the other.

*Imagine yourself surrounded by a shaft of white light. That
white light shines down from the heavens and anchors you into
the physical earth, yet you are far more than a physical being.
You are Awareness itself.*

*Take in a deep breath, imagining yourself inhaling the air
from above and below and pulling it into the heart. Allow it to
swirl around your entire energy field. Exhale longer than you
inhaled and feel yourself relaxing.*

*Take in another deep breath from above and below. Scan
the body as you slowly exhale. Release any tension, stress, and
any lower vibrations that no longer serve you.*

*Take in another deep breath, feeling the brain slow down
as you do so. Exhale slowly, and affirm that you are sinking,
deeper, deeper, and deeper into your chair.*

*Take a few moments now to lift your vibration as you
continue breathing slowly in and out, allowing your energetic
vibration to come into alignment with the flow of the Universe.*

*Breathing in, experience gratitude for whatever blessings in
your life come to mind. Breathing out, allow that gratitude to
fill every cell of your being, lifting your energy.*

With appreciation swirling throughout your field, see that high energy filling a sphere of light that surrounds you. With your intention, make that light brighter, brighter, brighter.

Depending on how you feel at this point, you may choose to use other tools to lift your energy or flow into the next stage. Maintain a state of excited anticipation of what your guide will share with you in each now-moment that follows, creating together the best and most wondrous experiences for the evolution of your soul and the evolution of the whole.

When you are feeling vibrant and totally relaxed, take a deep breath in preparation to expand your aura beyond its normal boundaries. Sense the borders of the spherical shape around your physical body. On the exhale, expand the sphere. Hear the outbreath like the wind in the trees as you dissolve into the field of all creation.

Affirm, "I . . . AM . . . limitless!"

Disengage now from identification with the contents of your human story by silently stating, "I surrender."

From this neutral state of being, imagine the level at which your main spirit guide exists.

Trust that at the soul level, you know exactly how to align to this frequency. Silently state, "Shift." Hold the intention to merge with your guide to help you and to serve the greatest possible good. Issue a heartfelt invitation such as, "Welcome . . . Come now."

Drawn to your attention by your light and by the love radiating from your heart, your guide senses this shift in your vibration, feels your invitation, and merges with you now in awareness.

Having prepared your energy field for this moment, spend as much time as you like experiencing whatever is meant to happen. Who is here? What do you feel? What do you know?

Turn up your awareness further, illuminating this field you have created with your love and gratitude. What do you sense now? What do you hear? What do you see?

Whether you sense a presence or not, fully engage this guide who will have responded by now to your invitation. Send thoughts such as, "Greetings, friend. What do you have to tell me? What is it I need to know?"

Any time that you feel you may have dropped the connection, or if you notice that you are no longer aware of a presence, slip back to simply being and shift again. Using all your soul senses, hear, see, and sense whatever unfolds.

Receive what is lovingly placed into your mind. Notice that words may not be necessary. Knowing can come in full bursts of awareness, and you can respond in kind.

When you sense that your time together has come to a natural conclusion, send a wave of gratitude for what has been received. Return to full waking consciousness energized, invigorated, and changed for the better because of what you have experienced.

Welcome back to the human focus. Center your awareness at the level of the heart and send love outward, knowing that you remain at all times fully connected with all that is.

PRACTICE:
THE SIP OF THE DIVINE

You may hear the word *meditation* and feel immediate resistance. The ego doesn't like taking a back seat to expanded states of consciousness.

Meditation is like exercise: it's good for you, it requires a regular routine to reap the rewards, and it takes dedication and commitment to maintain the benefits.

And just like exercise, most humans can find plenty of reasons not to do it.

Despite its transformative effects, the two most common excuses I hear from people for not meditating are, "I don't have the time" and "I can't quiet my mind."

There's another unspoken reason why many people don't maintain a regular meditative practice. They try it a few times and are frustrated when they don't sense anything out of the ordinary. They decide they are a failure at meditating and quit before giving themselves a chance.

The SIP of the Divine is a stunningly simple method given to me by my guides that resolves each of these challenges. It is easy to work into your daily routine, and it is an excellent method for taming the undisciplined monkey mind. It has the added benefit of allowing you to connect directly with nonphysical beings and receive guidance from a higher perspective. In other words, it hooks you up with your "genie in a bottle."

If you are like most people, you begin your day with a favorite beverage such as coffee, tea, or a breakfast smoothie. The time it takes you to prepare and take your first sip is probably three to five minutes. If you can set aside that much time each day for a beverage, surely you can find three minutes each day to SIP: *sit in peace*.

"SIP" is a play on words for this simple, yet effective practice that requires only three minutes from start to finish.

The "Divine" part of the meditation's name refers to the results. If you use these three minutes to regularly set your story aside and align with the higher dimensions, you will discover the heavenly treasures of peace, connection, guidance, and wholeness.

What are you waiting for?

Here's how to SIP:

- Sit or lie where you won't be disturbed.

- Set the timer on your smartphone for three minutes.

- Close your eyes and take one slow, deep breath to become relaxed and centered, exhaling longer than you inhale.

- Move awareness to the heart area and bring to mind something for which you are grateful. (This brings your heart and mind into alignment.)

- With the intention of aligning with the highest possible dimension from which answers to your questions and challenges will arise, silently state "Shift."

    o Note: As explained in detail for The BLESS ME Method, this step is equivalent to using the remote control to change the channel. You don't have to know how it

> works. Know that holding the
> intention and stating "Shift" will
> bring about the desired result.

- Trusting that wise, benevolent, nonphysical beings with a higher perspective are always available to help you, silently ask from the heart, "What do I need to know right now?"

- Sit peacefully and scan the field of awareness for an answer.

  o Note: Replies will come in the
  form of sensations, thoughts,
  images, or feelings. There is no
  need to know who is providing
  the response. What matters is
  whether the guidance is helpful.

- Engage anything of interest that arises in your mind. Ask follow-up questions as appropriate.

- If your mind wanders, do not resist the random thoughts. Shift back to being the clear sky of awareness observing the clouds that pass by.

- When the timer goes off, send a wave of gratitude for what has been received and open your eyes.

When you have done the practice enough times that you have a sense of how long three minutes is, try not using a timer. Honor any nudges from the soul and remain in the Power as long as you like.

"What do I need to know right now?" is an excellent question to ask anytime you have no specific challenges in your life. Feel free to change what you ask, but try to stick to only one question per session. The goal is to keep your mind relaxed. Follow-up questions are fine if you need clarity. For example, you could say, "What do you mean by that?" or "Why are you showing me that image?"

Hundreds of thousands of people have learned to enjoy this easy meditation. One woman, a kindergarten teacher, taught it to her students and the kids love it. They look forward to "sipping" every morning as a group and have shared it with their parents. Imagine how our world would change if everyone shifted their focus to soul awareness for just a few minutes each day.

Enter the practice with this same childlike excitement as the kindergarteners. After all, when you ask your "question of the day," you don't know what you don't know. Those with the higher perspective have your best interests at heart. They will often surprise you with unexpected answers.

Set the intention today to do The SIP of the Divine at least once a day for the next three weeks. It takes that long to create a new habit. You will find that this addition to your daily routine is so pleasurable and rewarding that you will want to continue the practice beyond the initial three-week period.

What a gift it is to deliberately spend three minutes daily in a state of wholeness, communing with Higher Consciousness. In so doing, you are aligning with your soul and reminding yourself you are not only human. This awareness will pay off throughout the day as you carry the energy of these precious moments with you.

PRACTICE:
THE BEST METHOD

There are any number of ways to move your awareness away from the contents of The Story of You and experience altered states of consciousness. Previous sections introduced two excellent practices to do so: The BLESS ME Method of connecting with Higher Consciousness and The SIP of the Divine.

In truth, you don't need any step-by-step method to connect with Higher Consciousness. The higher realms are here right now. The reason you aren't normally aware of the nonphysical dimensions and their inhabitants is because your focus is usually on your objective, physical experience.

As a soul, you are inseparable from the One Field of Awareness of which you are a part. To enjoy a clear and deliberate connection, it is vital to remove your focus from the objective world and place it on the subjective worlds.

The BEST Method is a quick, easy way to do this. The practice can be used in meditation, but it is not a meditation in itself. You can use it anytime and anywhere to feel connected, seek guidance, and speak with loved ones, guides, and angels.

Using this simple process ensures that you make the shift from the normal brain-based way you operate in Earth School to the soul-guided, heart-centered mode of interacting across dimensions.

Understand that you can ask questions or send thoughts to those in the nonphysical dimensions from your normal state of consciousness without using any process, and they will always be received. The BEST Method increases the possibility that you will hear or sense something in return.

BEST is an acronym to help you remember the four steps of this practice. The letters stand for *breathe, expand, shift,* and *trust.* While it is the fastest, easiest way to connect, it does have a few prerequisites. You must first do the following:

- Know what it feels like to be centered and be able to get centered quickly (that's the "Breathe" part).

- Understand what is happening when you make the *shift* in consciousness and know how to do it.

- Know how it feels to be in the soul's spacious state of being.

The BLESS ME Method and The SIP of the Divine will help you fulfill these requirements. Review and practice them until you feel confident that you are connecting with higher realms.

Once you are familiar with shifting between human and soul modes and you want to consciously interact with your guides or loved ones across the veil, you are ready to use The BEST Method. All you need to do is:

- Breathe—Take one slow, deep vagus breath to become relaxed and centered.

- Expand—Picture your aura moving outward to fill all space.

- Shift—Move your awareness from the head to the heart and from your human story to the spacious state of Wholeness.

- Trust—Know that you are a soul and that by making this shift you have optimized your ability to talk to guides, angels, and loved ones. Ask questions, receive guidance, bask in the presence of Love, and acknowledge your beautiful, shining light.

PRACTICE:
INSPIRED WRITING

———

In the days before e-mail and texting, people used to regularly write cards and letters by hand. The simple practice of sharing the written word engendered a sense of connection and focus that was maintained and intensified thanks to the time it took to put pen to paper.

You can use these benefits to your advantage today by engaging in written communication with those in the nonphysical realms. The recipients of such correspondence do not need you to write what you are thinking about for your thoughts to be known. They will appreciate your efforts for the reasons stated above, however, and will do their best to project their responses into your mind.

Some people refer to the practice of writing words from the higher realms as "automatic writing." This is not always an accurate description of what is occurring. In true automatic writing, you would be in a deep meditative state. You would make no conscious movement of your muscles, allowing those in the higher realms to direct your pen and form the words.

The practice of inspired writing is quite different. You deliberately write the words as you sense them rather than allowing a higher being to control your hand.

There are two types of inspired writing. In the first, those in Spirit gift you with beautiful, wise words to help you on your soul's journey. The words arise in your mind without thinking or trying. They may be in prose or poetry, personal or universal. The source is usually not a friend or family member but a helper of some kind. You play a passive role in this type of inspired writing, taking dictation directly from those in the higher realms.

The second type of inspired writing unfolds in conversational style. You usually have a sense of who you are interacting with. As you enjoy a mental dialogue, you write both sides of the conversation verbatim.

To engage in either type of experience, it helps to choose a time and place where you won't be interrupted. Sit with a pad of paper and a writing instrument that doesn't smear. You can write at a table or desk or lightly rest the paper on your lap. Alternatively, you can write on a device such as an iPad or laptop. If you choose the latter method, set the intention to remain in a right-brain state despite the use of electronics.

The BLESS ME Method is well suited for this practice. With the intention of doing inspired writing, go through the seven steps in the normal manner. The actual writing takes place in the final Experience step after the all-important Shift to the desired dimension and the invitation to merge.

If your intention is to connect with a specific person, guide, or angel, you can initiate the conversation. Otherwise, you may wish to sit quietly and wait to be inspired.

An excellent way to get the flow going is to write a question or words of greeting. You may keep your eyes closed as you write if this helps reduce distractions. In this case, use the feel of the paper against your hand to navigate the page. Don't be concerned about neatness or writing in a straight line.

Should you choose to open your eyes, maintain a soft, relaxed gaze. Don't focus intently on the words or worry about punctuation. Keep your attention on what is arising in your mind while maintaining a spacious, expanded state of awareness.

If you sense nothing at first, it is perfectly fine to write nonsensical words as you get started to get your left brain out of the way. Trust that those in spirit have responded to your invitation. Like a surfer catching a wave, they will merge with and flow into the thoughts you initially compose. As you continue writing, you will notice words arising that you would not have thought of.

Congratulations! You are being inspired.

At first the words may come haltingly or in brief spurts. With practice, you can get to the point where you are writing full sentences at your normal pace. Time will seem to stop as you relax into this connected state. Engage and interact. Your nonphysical writing partner has come to help you. Write everything you sense without filtering. At the end of the session, you will have a record of all that transpired.

When you return to your normal state of consciousness, be aware of the human tendency to doubt. Review what you have written and give it the heart test. Words from the higher dimensions carry a refined energy. Even though the thoughts received in inspired writing often sound like your own, you will sense a difference.

Do not give up after one or two sessions. Those in the nonphysical realms are waiting to work with you. When you show up for them, they will do their best to help you.

Was it helpful and healing? That is the bottom line.

WORKING WITH YOUR "A" TEAM

All beings are connected through the web of LIFE, but it's impossible to know and interact with everyone. Humans grow the most through relationships, and your family, friends, and colleagues serve this purpose well.

At the nonphysical level, you have a soul family with whom you go through multiple incarnations. Your loved ones from this current lifetime who have passed are part of this special group. You are always connected, whether they are in physical form or not. As we have discussed already, you also have guides who help you with the challenges of being human. And of course, there are greatly evolved intelligences whose task is to help all humanity.

Whether or not you sense the presence of your nonphysical family and helpers, trust that they are part of your personal energetic web. Hearing others' stories may help you believe in their existence, but nothing is more convincing than having your own NOE experience. That is the goal of this section.

We call these nonphysical family members and guides higher beings for several reasons:

- They operate at higher frequencies than you can perceive with your physical senses.

- They have a higher perspective of your life than you do.

- They can provide higher guidance that you may not be privy to unless you connect with their wisdom.

These beings do not exist at a separate level from you that is higher in a geographic sense. Their reality is energetic and interpenetrates this earthly one. Nevertheless, we refer to their dimension as being above our own. My friend, Dr. Gary Schwartz, a professor at the University of Arizona who conducts scientific research into the nature of consciousness, refers to the nonphysical beings who help us as our A Team, with "A" referring to *above*.

That makes you and me part of the B Team, with "B" referring to *below*.

Those on the A Team want you to know that they do not consider themselves superior to souls in human form. On the contrary. One of their major objectives is to help you understand that whether you experience yourself above or below, all are expressions of one Team arising within one infinite field of Awareness. In other words, it's all Joy!

The information and practices that follow will help you develop a closer relationship with your unseen helpers. You will learn how to validate that the experiences you have as you interact with your Team are not your imagination. You will also be able to notice and receive more easily the gifts they bring you.

It doesn't matter if you have previously limited your interactions to only those here in Earth School or you already know that angels and guides are very real. Here you will acquire tools and techniques to take your journey to the next level.

PRACTICE:
ENGAGING YOUR
HIGHER HELPERS

———

Even those who are not religious pray at some point in their lives. When faced with a major challenge, there is an instinctual reaction that causes humans to call out to something beyond the limited self for help. Many an atheist has admitted crying, "God, help me!" in a life-or-death situation. This instinctual act reveals the inner knowing that we are connected to a greater reality—that this life is not all there is.

Prayer is one form of connecting with Higher Consciousness. The type suggested in this section goes far beyond petitioning help in times of need. The practice of engaging your higher helpers is about maintaining a conscious, intentional, interactive, and highly personal relationship with beings you may have temporarily forgotten but have known for eternity.

If you've spent this lifetime like nearly everyone—unaware that you have an A Team—you can establish a conscious working relationship by using intention. Don't worry about why you haven't sensed them until now. That is a question you can ask them later using the tools and techniques in this book. Trust that you are on your unique path and your journey is unfolding perfectly.

With perfect timing, this book has found its way into your hands. As you open to your Team's existence, the higher beings who have your best interests at heart will make themselves known in a variety of ways:

- They may speak to you through thoughts that
  you will notice as you set the intention to
  be aware.

- You may perceive their presence now that
  you directly ask them to alert you with a
  noticeable sensation.

- You may receive wondrous signs that
  you can't explain away now that you are
  living lucidly.

- You may be led to just the right book, song
  lyrics, or person with the answers you seek.

You cannot fail to communicate with Spirit because you are already and always connected. No matter how your nonphysical helpers make themselves known, remember that these are creative, intelligent, sentient beings who are actively working with you. Engage in two-way interaction. Reach out to them often, responding and acknowledging anytime you sense a sign or message.

Be aware that the presence of those in Spirit can be very subtle, especially at first. Doubt is a sure way to diminish the signs. When first developing your awareness of your guides, embrace everything, no matter how subtle, no matter how unlikely the situation.

Send loving greetings from your heart. Transmit feelings of gratitude for higher beings' presence and assistance. Share your deepest desires, doubts, fears, and joys. Converse with them just as you would with a best friend, for indeed, they will fill such a role the moment you make space in your heart for them.

When you don't realize you have an A Team, you waste energy wondering how to deal with your challenges. With awareness, you can take your issues directly to those in the higher realms who always have the higher perspective. Feel this difference in the following two scenarios:

Option B: You pace back and forth, wringing your hands. You mutter aloud, "I don't know how to handle this situation. I just don't know what to do."

Option A: You sit quietly and take a vagus breath. You move awareness to the heart area and trust that you have an A Team of higher beings who know what you are dealing with. You hold the intention that the being with the best answer for you is near, and you ask (silently or aloud), "What do I need to know about this issue I'm dealing with? What is my best course of action?"

Option B is like shining a wide-beam flashlight around a dark room, looking for something you're not even sure is there. Option A directs a powerful laser beam onto the source of assistance.

Your A Team knows what will help you get the most out of your earthly experience. They will assist you to the best of their ability, but they will not interfere with a decision that you might need to make yourself. With the awareness that some of your greatest growth results from your free will choices, it is helpful to ask regularly that your lessons be as painless as possible.

The timing of your Team's responses will vary. You may receive an instant insight in response to your direct questions, or it might take several days until a meaningful sign appears. Because you ask clearly, you will notice when help arrives. Give thanks. This is a Team effort.

Your guides are here for you. They know you better than you know yourself. They enjoy being with you. They never judge you. There is nothing you can tell them that shocks or upsets them, nor is there anything that is too much trouble. They have your back.

With friends like this, you may want to optimize your relationship and do the following:

- Greet your Team first thing in the morning and when you turn out the light at night.

- Use The BLESS ME Method or The SIP of the Divine and talk with them in meditation.

- Ask for guidance or answers as needed using the abbreviated method in Option A above.

- Check in with them throughout the day to see if there's anything you need to know.

- Chat with them while driving, doing the dishes, or anytime you need a friendly ear.

- Send them an occasional burst of love and prepare to receive the same in return.

Engaging your guides in this manner will enhance your life in ways unimagined. Synchronicities will become a regular part of your life. Inspiration and creativity will flow, not by chance, but because you are actively aligning with the higher realms, trusting, and acting on the inner guidance sent your way.

In so doing, you will experience the peace that comes from knowing you are not alone. You will relax in the awareness that you don't need to handle your challenges all by yourself. In short, you will feel and know how very loved you are.

PRACTICE:
DISCERNING YES AND NO ANSWERS

From an early age, you learned to seek answers outside of yourself. You turned to family members, friends, teachers, and other experts when you needed advice or information. Depending on your age, you may have been encouraged to use an encyclopedia or a dictionary for research. Today, of course, the Internet is the go-to source for knowledge.

In the timeless dimensions, you have teachers, guides, and loved ones who are even closer at hand than Siri or Alexa. Once you discover how useful these ever-present helpers are, you may want to turn to them as your prime information resource.

Keep in mind that all are an expression of the One Mind. All answers and guidance ultimately arise from the same Source. Awareness will speak to you through apparently separate beings or via your soul's own inner knowing.

Data experts know that the easiest way to transmit information is via a simple binary system. The same is true when discerning answers to personal issues. Almost any question you might ask of Higher Consciousness can be worded in such a way that the answer is one of two responses: yes or no. This makes receiving guidance from the higher realms quite simple.

Your body and mind are intimately connected, and the body can't lie. This is the principle behind polygraph machines that measure changes in respiration, pulse, and blood pressure as indicators of deception.

You don't need machinery to detect a yes or no within the body. With intention and attention, you can discern subtle pressure, tightening, or tension that manifests in the solar plexus and chest if you ask a question for which the answer is no.

To try this for yourself, sit comfortably and take one or two vagal breaths. Move your awareness to the chest and solar plexus and notice how open and relaxed these two areas feel. Now, silently ask the question, "Was I born in 1902?" Notice the tension, however subtle, that arises in your torso as you ask a question for which the answer is a clear no.

If you don't feel a difference, do it again, paying close attention to the difference between how you feel before and after asking the question. (Be sure to recenter yourself with the breath each time you prepare to ask a question.)

Take another deep breath and clear your mind. Now ask silently, "Was I born in the year ____?" Fill in the blank with your correct birth year. Notice that when the answer to the question is yes, you maintain the open, relaxed, centered state.

You may feel this is a silly exercise. You know you weren't born in 1902. You know what year you were born. Yes, and the One Mind projecting as your Higher Self also knows this and transmits its knowing through the body.

Practice this technique several times with a variety of questions to which you know the answer, such as your age, occupation, and personality. Continue the exercise until you clearly sense a difference when the body says yes versus no. Again, be prepared for the subtlety when you are learning to attune to the body's signals. Be patient and persistent.

Be aware that if you have a lot of anxiety or you are emotionally involved with a certain issue, you may not be able to step far enough away from the story to receive trustworthy guidance. Do your best to become centered using the breath. Empty the mind as much as possible before asking any questions.

Take this practice to the next level by asking questions about issues that have an emotional element. Since this is for training purposes, make sure you know the answer to the questions, such as "Do I love my mother?" or "Am I compensated enough for my work?" See how emotional attachment affects the physical response, if at all.

When you can clearly discern a difference between yes and no in the body, move on to questions you don't know the answer to.

I once had a client call and ask if I could do a follow-up session for her. I told her that I was only taking new clients and asked why she felt she needed to come back. She told me that her deceased husband had clearly made his presence known during our first session. The details he provided about their life together allowed her to trust his messages from across the veil when he told her it was okay to marry again.

"I followed his advice," the woman said, "and I've been dating two very nice men in the year since our session."

I asked her why she felt a session with me would help. "Well," she said, "I can't decide which one to marry, and I want my husband to tell me."

I had to hide my amusement before I turned her down. I know from connecting with many of my clients' guides that those in the higher realms will not interfere when we face major life decisions such as marriage. Human beings learn best through trial and error. We are given free will to choose the actions most aligned with our best interests. Turning to outsiders to make decisions for you gives away your personal Power.

I explained to the woman that the body is beautifully designed to show us when we are deceiving ourselves. The heart is the bridge to the soul, and the soul knows what is best. Every client who has ever asked me for advice about a personal issue already knows the answer. They simply want validation.

I advised her to listen to her body, trust her heart, and act on what it told her.

Following this advice, she gave each man the heart test. The clenching she felt in her midsection as she imagined life with one or the other told her that neither was a good match at that time.

This simple exercise may have saved her a lot of anguish. It can do the same for you for big or little issues.

In addition to using the body as a barometer, you can devise a system of discerning yes/no answers from your Team in Spirit. Keep in mind that your guides and deceased loved ones are not all-knowing, but they do have a higher perspective than the limited human viewpoint.

They can advise you about issues such as the best timing to take action on decisions. They can help you find lost items when you word your questions so that they can be answered with a yes or no. They can show you the most helpful next steps in your life's journey.

Here's how to establish a reliable system of discerning yes/no answers from your A Team:

- Use The BLESS ME Method to go from normal waking consciousness to a relaxed, open, and expanded state of awareness. Set the intention of using this session to determine how your guide(s) will respond to questions that can be answered with a yes or no.

- When you reach the merge step, invite your main spirit guide to blend their consciousness with yours. Whether you sense a presence or not, trust that this merging has taken place.

- In the Experience/Engage step, empty your mind of all expectations and assumptions and silently ask your guide, "When I ask you a yes/no question, how will you communicate a yes response?"

- Notice the immediate sensation, thought, or feeling that arises in awareness. It could be a thought/word, a visual, or something you notice in your body.

- Thank your guide and empty your mind again.

- Ask silently, "When I ask you a yes/no question, how will you communicate a no?"

- Notice what spontaneously arises in awareness. In both cases, the symbol for yes and no could be something quite obvious or something completely unexpected.

- Thank your guide for this simplified way of communicating with your Team.

Ask that those in the higher realms use these new symbols with you from this moment forward when you need answers, validation, and reassurance. Feel the excitement that comes from trusting that they will.

You may wish to try out your new system with a few yes/no questions. Ask some for which you already know the answers and throw in a few issues you truly need help with. Notice how easily the correct symbol arises to an obvious yes or no. Trust these same symbols when they arise in response to questions that you truly want help with.

Don't just read the words of this exercise or think it through. This isn't about reading or thinking. Do the practice and see what results. The element of surprise is one of the prime ways that you come to trust this mode of communication as you personally experience the creativity and unexpected nature of A Team interactions.

As you relax and learn to trust your unseen helpers, you will no longer need to ask, "Are you really here?" The clear, open feeling in your heart will be all the answer you need.

PRACTICE:
ASKING FOR EVIDENCE

The most common question people ask about communicating with any aspect of Higher Consciousness is, "How do I know it's not my imagination?"

Discernment can be challenging because the thoughts, images, and emotions associated with multidimensional communication are perceived the same way as all other sensations, thoughts, and feelings: they bubble up in awareness.

Here's how to differentiate between your mind and that of a higher being (keeping in mind that all are shared experiences of the One Mind):

- You have an experience or sense information that is unexpected, that you didn't already know, or is not something you would have normally thought of.

- There is a strong emotional element to the interaction that you can't deny.

- You sense an unusual or unexpected physical sensation in your body.

- You have an experience in a dream that is much more solid and clear than your normal dreams, and it doesn't dissipate upon awakening.

- You simply know you're not making it up. Honor this.

Whether invited or unexpected, the best way to come to trust your interactions with higher beings is to ask them to prove their presence to you. They don't mind if you question the connection. They want you to know they are here.

The most immediate method of validation is to use the yes/no practice. Simply ask, "Is this you?" or "Can I trust what you just told me?" Sense the answer in your body or watch for your yes/no symbol. If you want a bit more certainty, you can ask whoever you are communicating with for evidence using any of the following three methods. Please do so with a childlike sense of wonder and enjoy the process. You are testing the connection, not challenging your beloved helpers.

1. **Ask, "What sign will you send me to validate this connection?"**

   Your nonphysical helpers can see where you are, where you're going, what you're doing, and what you are likely to experience in the next few days. When you ask what sign they will send to validate your communications, they answer with something they know from their higher perspective that you will encounter.

   Once you ask the question, clear your mind of all expectations and assumptions. Notice what immediately arises in awareness. Be alert for whatever stands out from your ordinary thoughts. The unspoken understanding when playing what I call *The Sign Game* is that the sign cannot be too ordinary nor too challenging. It will be something you wouldn't come across in a normal day, but it also won't be outrageously challenging, such as manifesting an object out of thin air.

I recently enjoyed a conversation with my stepdaughter across the veil. I had no doubt it was her, but I wanted my husband to trust the message I delivered to him on Susan's behalf. When I asked her what sign she would send me in the next day or two to validate this special visit, she put in my mind the image of a flying duck.

The next day, Ty and I went on a boat trip and docked at a marina we had never visited. Shortly after arriving, we took our dogs for a walk. As we passed some bushes at the end of the dock, one of our dachshunds startled a duck that had been nesting unseen in the foliage. She burst forth with a loud squawk and took off into flight directly in front of us. After I recovered from being startled, I laughed and said aloud, "Good one, Susan!"

Our boat trip had been planned for days. With her higher perspective in the astral realm, Susan knew of our plans. Physical matter is not solid to those in the nonphysical realms. Those across the veil can literally see through objects in our dimension, as Carly clearly demonstrated in an earlier chapter when she saw the dog biscuit beneath the sofa.

Susan would have seen the duck's nest along the route we took to go ashore. That duck flew out in front of us three more times during our brief stay at the marina, and each time I sent a wave of gratitude to Susan for giving us such great evidence that she is around us.

The more you play *The Sign Game*, the more you will realize that not all your thoughts are your own. I recently asked my main spirit guide what sign he would send me to validate an exchange we had during my morning meditation. He flashed the image of a watermelon in my mind. I couldn't remember the last time I had eaten or even seen a watermelon. I had no plans to go shopping in the next two days, so I knew this was random enough to make a good sign.

The whole day passed with no watermelon encounters. I noticed the appearance in my mind of a few human doubts that perhaps I had imagined the interaction with my guide, but I quickly dismissed them. I had successfully played *The Sign Game* often enough to know that signs show up in wondrous ways when you stop looking and put the game in the back of your mind.

An hour before bedtime, my husband unexpectedly announced he was going for a walk. He rarely does so at that time of the evening. Looking back, I have a hunch that some higher being put the thought in his head to stretch his legs at that unusual hour. As soon as he left, the thought arose in my mind to watch a little TV on my iPad. I rarely watch TV and can count on one hand the number of shows I had watched in the previous six months.

I was drawn to watch an episode of *20/20*—a program I had not viewed in years. In retrospect, it is clear there was a higher mind gently guiding me. At the time, however, even knowing that our guides are always present, I felt all the thoughts were my own.

Five minutes into the news program, a guest on the show declared, "Everybody knows our town is famous for one thing: our *watermelon* festival." My body convulsed in joyous surprise, and I gaped at the image of a wall-sized mural of a watermelon on my screen.

For the next few minutes I was pummeled with one picture after another related to watermelons as the man discussed their festival. I laughed with joy as I took multiple screenshots to memorialize this magical moment.

I have played *The Sign Game* often enough to know that this was no chance encounter. I was led thought by thought to this beautiful validation of our interconnectedness. As you play the game, you will enjoy "That's my sign!" moments and feel the knowing that accompanies these validations from Spirit.

2. **Ask the higher beings to share a current event in the life of someone you know.**

As you make this request, hold in mind a person with whom you will be able to validate whatever the higher being shares with you. Just as in *The Sign Game*, clear your mind and notice the first thing that arises in awareness. It can bubble up as an image, a word, a sentence, a sound, or a feeling in your body.

Thank whoever it is you are communicating with. Next, contact the person here in physical form to whom the information relates. Tell them you are trying to validate a current event related to them that was put in your mind. It will help if they are open to transdimensional communication, as they can celebrate with you when they affirm that what you perceived is correct.

I play this game often with my friend Brenda across the veil to check my attunement with higher beings. I ask her to tell me something that our mutual friend Lynette is currently doing or has done in the last 24 hours or so. The images and messages she sends are stunningly accurate, showing that those across the veil are aware of our day-to-day activities and even our thoughts.

A remarkable example of the web in action occurred one day when I was preparing to help a client connect with her departed loved ones. I shifted my focus to Brenda and asked her to tell me something going on with Lynette to validate that I was properly prepared for my upcoming session. Instead of telling me about Lynette, Brenda told me that our mutual friend Jayne was going through a rough patch.

I hadn't communicated with Jayne in at least a year. I passed along this message from Brenda to Lynette and asked her to find out what was going on with our friend.

Lynette texted Jayne while I conducted my session. She learned that Jayne was, indeed, dealing with some challenges. Unbeknownst to Lynette or me, Jayne—who knew about this game Lynette and I play—had silently asked Brenda for a favor. She wanted Brenda to mention her struggles the next time Lynette and I played *The Sign Game*.

This four-way connection is unprecedented. Brenda knew what neither Lynette nor I did, and she used the two of us to provide comfort and reassurance to her friend Jayne. What a wondrous way to validate that all of us have the full support of those in the ethereal realms!

3. **Ask for any factual information that you don't know.**

Take advantage of your A Team's access to the Cosmic Web by asking them to share something you can validate on the World Wide Web. This is as simple as silently saying, "I trust that this is you. To validate your presence, please tell me something I don't know."

Just like the two methods above, once you ask the question, immediately empty your mind. Those you are communicating with will put a thought or image into your mind. Send gratitude for whatever you perceive, then go online and do your research.

I played this game once when I decided to see if I could connect with the spirit of Albert Einstein. I clearly felt a distinct personality and heard his voice, complete with German accent. Admittedly, it was initially challenging for my human side not to wonder if I was imagining the conversation. The more we interacted, the more information he gave me. The two-way dialogue showed me that I was not simply pulling data from a lifeless field of information.

When we had finished interacting, I did a Google search for each of the items Professor Einstein had shared with me during that special visit. All of it proved correct, including jobs he held before he became famous and details about his family members. He even led me to a specific image of himself on the cover of *Time Magazine*. That particular issue had the highly appropriate title: "Rediscovering Einstein."

May you come to rediscover your real-time interconnectedness with the higher realms by using these methods. Over time, you will no longer need to ask for evidence to validate the connections. You will have come to know the truth of who you are and choose to interact in this playful way for the sheer Joy of it!

PRACTICE:
NOTICING SNAGS AND PULLING THE THREAD

———

Your nonphysical helpers are so present with you that their individual energies are part of your everyday awareness. This makes it easy to overlook them. You may not yet see, hear, or be consciously aware of them, so they may communicate important messages using what I call "snags."

To snag something means to become entangled. Your mind is eternally entangled with all others as part of the One Mind. If you are willing to let your higher helpers get a message through to you by catching your attention, they will snag you with anything that passes through your awareness.

Like a snag on a wool sweater, mental snags from Higher Consciousness stand out from everything else. You know better than to pull a loose thread on a good sweater, but you definitely want to pull the thread on a snag from your A Team.

Once you understand how these special attention-getters feel and function, you will learn to pause and focus on that snag. You then silently ask, *Why did you catch my attention with this?* Pay attention to what you sense in response. If it's helpful, act on it. Trust me, you'll be glad you did, and you will soon come to know how very guided and cared for you are.

To begin using snags as a communication device with your Team, move your awareness to the heart area. With the belief that there are higher beings who will hear and help you, ask them to clearly snag your attention from now on anytime they have something helpful to share.

Do it now, directing your request to loved ones across the veil, to guides, and even to higher beings. After encouraging them to make every effort to gain your attention, send them gratitude for the help you will receive from this useful practice.

You don't have to be consciously looking for snags throughout the day. Now that you have asked your Team to snag you, they will do so even when you aren't thinking about them.

To give it a try, take a relaxing breath and look around you. Soften your gaze and scan your entire field of vision slowly from left to right. Notice how your attention moves with your eyes, flowing like a paintbrush over all the objects you perceive. At some point as you gaze around, you will pause ever so slightly on one object for no apparent reason. You'll start to keep moving your eyes forward, but you'll find yourself slightly fixated on the object where you paused. That is a snag.

Stop scanning now and focus directly on whatever it is that caught your attention. Move your awareness to your heart and silently ask of Higher Consciousness, *Why did this snag me?* It is not important to know who snagged you. Simply clear your mind and notice what arises in response to your question. Your Team will use the object that snagged you to deliver a meaningful message. For example:

- As you gaze around your living room, you are snagged by a plant. You ask Higher Consciousness why the plant snagged you. A memory of the time you gave your mother a similar plant for Mother's Day unexpectedly arises in your mind. You experience a wave of love and know that your mother is thinking of you. Take this opportunity to Engage and talk with her!

- You are snagged by a deck of tarot cards sitting on a shelf. You tune in and sense that you are being guided to select one card from the deck. You do so, and it validates a major decision you recently made.

- You are snagged by a song playing on the radio. When you "pull the thread" and ask why this song caught your attention, you notice that the lyrics are the precise words your loved one across the veil used to say to you. Send them a loving thank you and *Engage* in conversation.

- You are driving on the highway and a billboard—one out of dozens you have passed—snags your attention. You read the words and realize they directly answer a question you asked your guides earlier. Send them a wave of gratitude.

It is eye-opening when you realize how easily you can now receive messages and connect across the veil. Not surprisingly, the more you notice these oh-so-subtle attention-grabbers, the more your Team will use them.

Be aware from moment to moment. Working with snags is a fun, wondrous, and highly practical way to build an ongoing, interactive relationship with those who have your best interests at heart.

PRACTICING PRESENCE MOMENT BY MOMENT

If you want to see what presence looks like, watch a new baby in its crib. It gazes about, taking everything in. It will stare, mesmerized, at a mobile overhead. It smiles in reaction to the beaming faces looking back at it. It cries when the body sends painful reminders that it's time to eat or drink. It is very much present because all it knows is "now."

You may have more difficulty remaining present. You have accumulated countless experiences since your time in a crib, and all of them together make up "The Story of You." Even though the rest of your story has yet to unfold, if you are like most humans, you predict the future based on the past.

This poses a challenge because humans are hardwired to notice the negative. This is a leftover self-protective mechanism from the days of cavemen. It's good to be vigilant, but the tendency to focus on your problems keeps you from being present. Instead, the mind dwells on the painful past and frets about the fearful future.

Being present can be challenging because you are conditioned to run from pain, whether physical or emotional. It is wise to run or take other appropriate action when there is a clear threat to your safety and well-being. The problem is that most people resist, deny, ignore, and avoid anything that is less than pleasant. The result is a feeling of emptiness that leads to unhealthy choices and addictive behavior.

When you do think about the present, it's mostly about the elements of your story, especially as they compare to other people's stories. You may worry: Am I successful enough? Do I look okay? Does anyone care about me? It's no wonder most people feel scattered and incomplete. The concept of wholeness is lost in the fragments of the past, present, and future story.

There is a vast difference between focusing on the present and being present. To be present is to be aware from an Observer's point of view of the sensations, thoughts, and feelings arising here and now. You notice what arises, but you don't automatically and mindlessly identify with what shows up.

This mental distancing allows you to:

- Be aware of the ST-F that stands out from your normal, conditioned ways of thinking, doing, and being.

- Enjoy experiences and obtain information you might otherwise have missed.

- Stop repeating conditioned behavior.
- Make higher choices aligned with Love.
- Find peace no matter what is happening in the present moment.

The Earth School experience is about dancing and flowing with the entire spectrum of possibilities. This includes all opposites: what humans consider the bad as well as the good, the painful as well as the pleasant. It is through contrast that you learn and grow and find the greatest Joy.

There is no downside to being present.

When you no longer deny your wholeness, you will experience the fullness of LIFE, warts and all. The practices that follow will allow you to make the most of every moment. Some help you to *experience* presence; others are tools that *require* presence. They are combined here purposefully, for when practiced regularly, they provide you the gift of finally feeling fully alive.

B-P-M PRACTICES

The heart has long been associated with love and connection. To be heart-centered is to enjoy a life focused on
loving relationships with others. Energetically, the heart
chakra is the balance point between the three lower, more
earthly energy centers and the three higher, more spiritual
chakras. For this reason, the heart is considered the bridge
between heaven and earth, the balance point between
your human persona and the soul.

The beating of the heart is one of the prime indicators of life in the physical body. Its rhythm is described
in beats per minute, a measurement that medical person-
nel abbreviate as BPM. I introduce this acronym here as a
handy way to remember three valuable tools to maintain
presence. In this case, the letters stand for breathing, posture, and mindfulness.

Each is a simple practice to implement into your daily
life. They can be done together or separately when you
feel disconnected or anytime you want to consciously be
in the "now."

Ironically, it requires presence to notice when you
most need to practice presence. Here are steps for setting
the intention to become aware when you are out of balance or stressed:

- Close your eyes.
- Take one to three vagal breaths to
  get centered.
- Move awareness from the head to the heart.

- Connect in awareness with your A Team.

- Send forth the strongest possible intention to become aware when your mental, emotional, and physical states are not peaceful.

- Ask for your Team's assistance in snagging your attention if you have lost awareness.

- Send a wave of gratitude and feel a surge of excitement at this new way of being.

From this moment on, with the slightest awareness that you are stressed, you can choose one or all of the following B-P-M practices to regain your center.

BREATHING

The breath serves as a point of focus when your mind is scattered. Breathing slowly and deeply calms the body when you are tense. One vagal breath can instantly bring you to a point of balance. Once peaceful and centered, you may continue focusing on the breath to maintain a higher perspective of "The Story of You."

POSTURE

Energy flows where consciousness goes. When you are stressed, anxious, or feeling any other constricting emotion, the body mirrors this energy by curling inward. Just for a moment, allow yourself to experience sadness or grief. Notice what you feel in the body. Please pause and do this.

Your head likely rolled forward and your shoulders slumped. You felt a tightness in the heart.

Now feel joy. Please make the bodily motions you equate with joy.

What happened? You likely uncurled and sat taller. If you really got into the feeling, you couldn't help but raise your arms to the heavens.

In doing the B-P-M practice, you consciously and deliberately assume the posture of joy and positivity. With the intention of feeling centered and connected to Higher Consciousness, you hold your head high and put your shoulders back, and in so doing, you open your heart to the Universal flow.

Do it now and feel the Power that instantly flows more freely through your being.

Using the steps above to practice presence, pause and set the intention that from now on, assuming this open posture will remind you that you are always and already connected to Higher Consciousness. When you get out of bed first thing in the morning, put your shoulders back and send a loving greeting to your Team. Throughout the day, as you become aware that your body has slipped back into a more inward posture, open again and smile as you do so. You are conscious and connected!

Notice how insights arise and synchronicities become commonplace as you use posture to live The Awakened Way!

MINDFULNESS

Presence is a state. Mindfulness is a practice. It is similar to presence in that you are paying attention to what is here and now instead of allowing the mind to wander to the past or future. With mindfulness, however, you make a conscious effort to remain present.

Mindfulness is a way of life that requires some effort. Without mindfulness, you can easily get stuck in the conditioned ST-F of your story. When you regularly practice mindfulness, you experience yourself as part of the flow of LIFE, receiving insights and guidance you might otherwise miss.

As you become aware of moving from one action to the next without pause, stop for a bit and simply be. Put your shoulders back, breathe deeply, and send a wave of gratitude to the Higher Self for this moment of awareness and clarity.

Use these B-P-M moments to reconnect with your Team. There's no need to drop into meditation to communicate with your nonphysical helpers. Simply shift Awareness to a higher channel anytime, anywhere and send them a greeting.

You can use these conscious connections to ask for guidance about a current issue. The most helpful question at any time is, "What do I need to know right now?"

Remain SILENT and LISTEN (notice that these two words contain the same letters). You may receive an answer in the form of a sensation, thought, or image that stands out from your normal ST-F.

No matter what you sense, what you experience in these sacred time-outs is presence, which leads to peace. What you experience is This . . . your essential nature. Take these brief breaks often to recharge, refresh, and remind yourself you are more than your story.

Your heart beats in reliable BPMs in your chest, powered by an unseen force that loves you beyond measure. Use the B-P-M practices as opportunities to develop an ongoing relationship with this Higher Self and all its many projections.

AWAKENED WAY
REMINDERS

———

You have spent a lifetime focusing on The Story of You. The habit of identifying with yourself as a separate "me" or "I" rather than as Aware Awareness becomes ingrained. You may have a powerful awakening that leaves no doubt Who you are, yet you still slip easily back into the story.

It may take time and effort to overcome your human conditioning and to integrate awareness of your Higher Self into your day-to-day thoughts and actions. One way to make the process easier is by using physical world attention-getters to remind you to shift beyond the material world.

You may be familiar with the saying "Out of sight, out of mind." Because the subtle realms are generally out of sight, you can remain consciously connected to the greater reality by leaving visual cues well in sight.

I use all the following reminders, and I know they will help you as well:

- Wear a symbolic bracelet, wristband, or ring. Set the intention as you put it on that each time you become aware of it, you will focus on your multidimensional nature. In these moments of presence, you can:

- o Send a loving greeting to your Team.

- o Ask a question for which you're seeking an answer.

- o State a positive affirmation about your new Awakened Way of living.

- o Practice B-P-M.

Note that if you wear a piece of jewelry on the same arm or finger for more than a couple of days, it will no longer stand out in awareness. To counter this, switch it to the other arm or hand every few days so that it continues to snag you.

- Put meaningful objects or pictures in places where you will see them often. Good locations include:

- o Next to the sink where you brush your teeth

- o Hanging from your car's rear-view mirror

- o Beside your computer

- o Hang a chalkboard where you will see it often and write Awakened Way reminders on it. Change your affirmative phrases often.

- Send yourself an e-mail with a subject line that reminds you to remain awake and aware. When you get used to seeing it in your inbox, delete that e-mail and write a fresh one. Examples for your chalkboard and e-mails include:

o   I am not only human.

o   I am so very loved.

o   I AM.

o   Add your own visual Awakened Way reminder here: _____

_____

_____

For auditory prompts, there are apps for your smartphone or watch that will send you random alerts such as a bell or chime. Each time you hear the sound, use this to send a greeting and check in with your Team of Light beings. If the auditory dings and chirps are too intrusive, set the app to leave a silent notification on your screen.

My Awakened Way app for smartphones sends push notifications each day when I post the latest daily message. These inspiring words are a great way to counteract the media's emphasis on negative news and remind you of your innate goodness.

There is no limit to the creative ways you can integrate awareness of your multidimensional nature into your day-to-day life. For example, when someone near you sneezes, add a greeting to your guides along with the "God bless you" or "Gesundheit" response that most of us are conditioned to say.

During a period of several years when I experienced hot flashes, I transmuted those unwelcome visitors from an irritant to a spiritual tool. After setting a clear intention, each time I felt the familiar rush of heat coming on, instead of complaining, I remembered to state positive affirmations and consciously connect with Higher Consciousness.

Now that's integration!

Be creative. Ask your guides to give you unique ways to increase your connection with them. Anything you can do to shift your attention from the limited story to your spacious, flowing Self is well worth the effort.

THE HUMAN/SOUL DIAL

___

While you are here in Earth School, you as Aware Awareness experience the full spectrum of states of consciousness. These flow from limited human consciousness through the spacious awareness of the soul to pure *Being*.

You may go through periods when you remain in an expanded state of knowing you are more than your physical body, and then you swing back the other way to thinking, feeling, and acting "fully human."

To live The Awakened Way is a balancing act. The goal is to find the sweet spot moment by moment somewhere in the middle between left brain and right brain, between the head and the heart, between human nature and true nature.

An excellent tool to help with this goal is to visualize your states of being on a dial much like a traditional fuel tank gauge. Instead of E for empty on one side and F for full on the other, picture a dial that swings between H for human and S for spirit.

Using mindfulness, practice presence throughout your day and tune in to your thoughts, feelings, and actions. As you become aware of your state of consciousness, judge where you are on the H/S Dial.

I recall a day when my husband and I were traveling through Northern California. I was at the wheel of our large RV in rush hour traffic outside San Francisco. With 46,000 pounds of mass, our bus did not stop quickly.

I was holding the wheel firmly, doing my best to stay focused, when a car came zipping up beside us. The driver abruptly cut in front of the bus only inches from our front bumper. Reacting automatically, one of my hands flew off the wheel, and I made an R-rated gesture you might recognize!

Sitting in the passenger seat, my husband did a double take, then shouted, "Yes!" as he pumped a fist and added, "She's human!"

It only took a moment for me to regain awareness and sense the difference between my human nature and my more spacious self. I smiled sheepishly, aware in that instant that the arrow on my H/S Dial was pegged to the H side. I brought myself easily back to the center by using the phrase, "Isn't that interesting!"

Occasionally, it feels good to be fully human. However, because you are also a soul who is fully Spirit, there is a knowing when it's time to swing back toward the center.

Free will is the gift that allows you to find the middle ground between Human and Spirit at any time. This results in a balanced state, evidenced by greater feelings of love, peace, and compassion no matter what is going on around you. With practice in using the H/S Dial, you will come to enjoy moderation through presence.

SILENCE ON THE BRIDGE!

I have been a sailor my whole life, and I have seen how boating mirrors the human experience. Due to multiple variables interacting at any given time, such as wind, current, and speed, navigating a boat requires highly focused attention. It is certainly enjoyable to spend time on the water, but the peace is often punctuated with moments of high drama.

Any activity that demands your total attention helps you to practice presence. In the state of flow that arises when you are focused and alert, you transcend all sense of time and place. Without the distractions of the past, the future, or "The Story," you experience an invigorating sense of being fully alive.

One of my more memorable experiences on a boat led me to the practice in presence that I call "Silence on the Bridge." The technique is an astoundingly simple yet highly effective method for quieting your inner critic and getting in the flow.

Ty and I had just taken possession of a trawler that we named *Gratitude*. Her previous owner, "Dave," graciously volunteered to get underway with us for a day to show us idiosyncrasies about the boat that we couldn't learn from the manuals.

As we prepared to leave the slip, I whispered to Dave that he might see a different side of my husband during our outing. "Ty is in total mission mode today," I cautioned him, "so don't take it personally if he's a little curt."

Dave casually waved off my warning, and the three of us gathered in the boat's wheelhouse. The well-equipped bridge was one of the things Ty and I liked best about our new boat. It was the closest thing to being back aboard the bridge of a destroyer that Ty had experienced since he retired from the Navy.

Knowing that I had never maneuvered a boat with twin engines, Ty offered me the chance to get *Gratitude* underway for the first time. I eagerly took the helm with the two men flanking me. I found it quite easy to pull out of the slip, but an opening drawbridge a short distance ahead soon demanded my full attention.

Dave did not seem to notice my need to focus. He chose that moment to start sharing a rather lengthy family story. I could feel Captain Ty bristling at the distracting chatter that went on and on. Suddenly reverting to his Navy training, Ty startled both Dave and me by barking sternly, "Silence on the bridge!"

The words did the job, effectively stopping Dave mid-story. I glanced over my shoulder and communicated an "I told you so" with my eyes. We enjoyed complete silence until I brought the boat safely through the drawbridge.

Later, we had a good laugh at the way Ty's Navy training kicked in during a stressful moment. Happily, Silence on the Bridge proved to be the perfect name for the useful tool I discovered later while bringing *Gratitude* into our marina.

Getting into our new slip requires some tricky maneuvering. I found myself in full-blown human ego mode the first two times I brought her back to port. The inner chatter about what might go wrong caused me to tense up and overcorrect.

It's said that the third time's a charm, and in my final effort I was given a gift. It came in the form of an inner voice guiding me to flatten my tongue against the roof of my mouth during the tense moments. Eager to reduce the stress, I pressed my tongue upward, molding it to my palate.

The distracting "what if" thoughts that had held me in a state of anxiety instantly disappeared. I found the inner silence stunning and the lack of tension utterly freeing.

Without the disruptive voice of my ego, I was able to hear and follow the intuitive guidance that is always present, and I made the best landing yet. The greatest gift of all was that without the fear, I had immense fun maneuvering the boat in the tight quarters and wanted to do it over again!

How can something as simple as pressing your tongue against the roof of your mouth be so effective? As my guides later explained, the movement connects the two major energy meridians in the body, thus completing a critical circuit.

Ancient practices of energy medicine suggest that the Central Meridian runs up the front of your torso and ends in the center of your lower lip. It is a conduit for yin, or feminine, energy. The Governing Meridian runs up your spine and neck, continues up and over your head and down the face, ending in the center of your upper lip. It is a conduit for yang, or masculine, energy.

When you flatten your tongue against the roof of your mouth, you energetically unite the Central and Governing Meridians. Ego survives on feelings of separation. As you bring yin and yang together with the tongue, you allow your vital energies to flow in a full circle. When you achieve this state of wholeness, the result is instant "silence on the bridge."

You are a being of Light. The Universe supports all your positive efforts. The next time you have to do anything that makes you nervous, press your tongue to the roof of your mouth and observe what happens.

Don't curl your tongue or point it. Simply raise it naturally and gently press it against the palate. If you are involved in an activity that lasts more than a few minutes, the tongue may return to its normal resting position, and you may need to repeat the motion as needed.

I shared this technique with a friend while we were traveling on a busy highway. I had no idea that passing tractor trailers was a major stressor for her. She tried this new tool several times while changing lanes and happily announced, "It works!"

What would you do if you knew you couldn't fail? It makes no difference if the tasks you face are physical or mental. Your ego doesn't want you to find out how gracefully you can sail through life when fear isn't a factor, for then you would harness your true Power and become a master manifester.

To protect its role, ego puts thoughts of failure and doubt into your mind at every opportunity. Remember: ego is no-thing. It is simply a pattern of conditioned human thinking.

Use the Silence on the Bridge practice anytime you notice ego's voice overriding the still, small voice within. With presence, you will feel ever more guided. In place of insecurity, you will experience newfound confidence. The contrast between mental noise and silence is blissful, indeed.

TURNING EMOTIONAL SCARS INTO GLOWWORMS

You may remember me sharing how my friend Brenda came to visit me within hours of crossing the veil. The evidence she provided to validate her presence let us know that she was far from dead and gone.

Brenda explained to me in those fascinating first visits the reason she was able to communicate so clearly and so quickly after her physical body's death. Her lucidness was the result of having done her inner work. She had cleared away enough human conditioning to be fully awake and aware of her true nature when her body died.

She was the first to admit that a lifetime of self-loathing had taken its toll. She was ultimately unable to cure her cancer, but through her own hard efforts, she healed her emotional wounds. By the time she transitioned, she had no doubt that she was worthy of love.

A retired teacher, Brenda wasted no time sharing the wisdom derived from her new higher perspective as a disembodied soul. Some of the greatest pearls provide the perfect summation of this final section of the book:

Most people are walking wounded, Suzanne. You can see the scars from up here. They're like little knife wounds all over the auras. But don't worry. They're battle scars, and that inner light never does go out. Just like you always say, we really are the Light.

The wounds that you don't work on fester. But the scars that are healed by working on them get this extra light around them. They look like little glowworms.

Could there be any more beautiful imagery to show that you are not alone in your human struggles and that your efforts to raise your consciousness truly make a difference?

There is great truth in the phrase, "what you feel you can heal." The practices that follow will help you shine a light on your battle scars and, like Brenda, heal them from the inside out.

THE NO FAULT PROCESS

Your natural attributes as a soul include loving kindness, caring, and compassion. Earth School allows you to express these at will along with all other possible states, including the less desirable ones. Being human, you are no stranger to feelings of guilt, anger, fear, shame, loneliness, unworthiness, doubt, and insecurity.

Negative feelings stand out in sharp contrast to your essential nature and thus can be quite uncomfortable. Humans tend to run from pain. It is common to resist, ignore, or stuff down anything that doesn't feel good.

Unfortunately, repressed feelings carry an energetic charge. Pent-up emotions can turn you into the equivalent of a simmering pot with a lid on it. Unless you create an outlet for all that heat, you will eventually boil over. Some common toxic human behaviors are listed in the introduction to this book. There's no need to dwell on them. You are probably all too familiar with how you react to pressure.

Don't feel bad. Disharmonious feelings are part of your wholeness. Your soul knows that you are a masterpiece in the making. All good paintings have a mix of dark and light. It is the contrast that makes a work of art more beautiful.

When you become aware that your emotions are being triggered, there are specific actions you can take to let off steam and stop the simmering once and for all. The NO FAULT process is one such practice. It is designed to realign your human story with your true nature.

The seven letters stand for *notice, observe, feel, acknowledge, uncover, love,* and *talk*. Each of these verbs represents consecutive steps that allow you to vent pent-up thoughts and emotions, honoring and integrating any earthly experience, no matter how painful.

When my guides gave me the acronym for this practice, I googled "no-fault divorce" to make sure I understood the meaning of the term. As I did so, I turned to Ty and said, "Honey, if you happen to see this page open on my computer, don't worry. I'm just doing a little research for my teaching. Our marriage is fine!"

I discovered that the term is perfectly suited for this process. In a no-fault divorce, there is no need to prove wrongdoing by any party. Similarly, when something triggers repressed ST-F in you that needs to be released, it serves no purpose to blame anyone.

Most of your wounds are the result of interactions at an early age with other wounded people. The NO FAULT practice recognizes this. It does not entail blaming yourself, your parents, teachers, or anyone else who influenced you in your formative years.

This lack of judging or blaming is critical, for *you are most likely to heal your story when you can see beyond it.*

Here are the seven steps that will help to transform your scars into glowworms:

N-OTICE whenever any uncomfortable human thoughts, feelings, or behaviors that you wish to transmute arise within you. This requires a commitment to being aware.

O-BSERVE these human thoughts, feelings, or behaviors with interest and curiosity. You do this by shifting your focus to be the neutral and compassionate Observer. This is the soul's natural perspective. Step back mentally and say or think, "Isn't that interesting!"

F-EEL fully the emotions that your body is processing without the need to label these feelings "wrong" or "bad" or to believe that whatever you are feeling shouldn't be happening. Simply be present, taking no action to sedate your emotions or to control the situation. Watch how the feelings flow through you without getting stuck as you simply feel them and don't take ownership of them.

A-CKNOWLEDGE from the soul's perspective that these feelings and this experience are perfectly valid aspects of your wholeness as a human being, no matter how unpleasant.

U-NCOVER the root cause of your human discomfort. Ask Higher Consciousness what happened to you as a child that caused the current situation to be uncomfortable for you now. Stay present with what arises, continuing to O-bserve, F-eel, and A-ckowledge what *is*. Hold the intention of gaining further insights in the days ahead about the dynamics that have caused this discomfort.

L-OVE your human self from your limitless Higher Self's perspective without any conditions. No matter how loving (or incapable of loving) your parents may have been, be the ideal parent now to your wounded human self. Caress your cheek or wrap your arms around yourself with genuine compassion and understanding. Give your human side the attention and love it craves.

T-ALK to yourself with the Voice of the Divine Presence that is always and already here. Use heartfelt phrases that will convey healing to your human side, such as:

- "You are safe."
- "I am here for you now and always."
- "I love you and will always love you without any conditions."

- "You are fine exactly as you are. You are not damaged. You are worthy."
- "I am here to nurture you. There is no need to fear anything."

Set aside any earthly feelings of self-consciousness and address yourself from the loving, nonjudgmental openness of the soul. You might give that wounded inner child a feel-good nickname to better appreciate this important difference in perspective. Your conversation might go something like this:

I promise you, sweetheart (substitute your nickname here), that I, your Higher Self, am going to parent you . . . to lovingly nurture you, to pay attention to you, to appreciate you, to listen to you, to hear you, and to love you unconditionally. I will validate all your emotions and experiences. I assure you that I will not frighten, intimidate, or judge you. Instead, I am here to make sure you feel safe always, no matter what.

Do this process regularly and you will be far less reactive to what has triggered you in the past. You will start to make healthier, more loving choices as you come to know peace from the inside out and experience the bliss of unconditional self-love.

UPLEVELING
YOUR POINT OF VIEW

———

Ego is the default mode for human beings. The ego survives and thrives when you identify yourself as a stand-alone being and adopt a "me against the world" mindset. Ego loves making comparisons. Other people's successes become a cause for envy and generate personal feelings of "not good enough."

Your identification with yourself as a human being is a highly limited perspective of Pure Consciousness. The soul's point of view is far more spacious and unitive. As you awaken, negative thoughts and egoic behaviors contrast so sharply with the soul's bright light that you clearly notice when you are out of alignment. It is in these moments of awareness of your true nature that you can pause and shift your point of view higher.

In releasing your identification with the ego, you realign with the soul and find instant peace. Better yet, you come to know yourself beyond the soul—as pure *Being*—and from this state enjoy the knowing that all is well, no matter what.

This is spiritual shape-shifting at its best. It will instantly transform any human interaction or situation.

Here is an example of how you might uplevel your perspective when ego tries to dominate your thoughts and actions:

- You receive an e-mail from a friend who works in the same field as you do. Your friend tells you that she has been given a chance to put her skills to use in an exciting new way. You have worked as hard as she has, and this is an opportunity that you had hoped to earn for yourself.

- Your immediate reaction is envy. You find it difficult to be happy for your friend.

- Because you have been practicing lucid living, you are aware of experiencing uncomfortable feelings.

- You recognize your reaction as coming from the ego. Instead of berating yourself, you see this as a chance to uplevel to the soul's point of view.

- With intention, you move into your heart space and shift to soul awareness. From this higher perspective, you know that you and your friend share the same Source. With this recognition, your envy dissolves, and you feel happiness for your friend's success.

- Still identifying with yourself as a soul, you realize that there is an even higher point of view you can assume. With total lucidity, you uplevel one more time to the perspective of Wholeness.

- Now seeing the situation through the eyes of Unity, you realize that you and your friend not only share the same Source, you *are* Source. In This-Awareness, your friend's success becomes your success.

- You notice that all envy and tension are gone, replaced with Joy.

This teaching has been shared in various forms for millennia. One of the most revered epic poems in Hindu literature, the *Ramayama*, conveys the concept of changing perspectives via a conversation between Lord Rama and the character Hanuman. Rama is a high-level deity, and he asks how Hanuman perceives him.

Hanuman responds that when he believes himself to be the body, he sees himself as Rama's faithful servant. Hanuman then shifts his consciousness upward. He acknowledges that when he knows he is a soul, he sees himself as a spark of Rama's Divine Light. And then, in a display of total lucidity, Hanuman declares that when he aligns with Truth, he knows that he and Rama are one and the same.

Hanuman's answer is the true essence of "upleveling."

Practice shifting your point of view higher by two levels in your varied human interactions, and you will come to know this truth as well. Your soul is already aware of your Divinity. As you raise your awareness to the higher states of the Self, ego will have no choice but to dissolve.

What a blessing this simple practice is, for when you experience the lack of separation between yourself and others, you will come to know yourself as Love.

FORGIVENESS IN AN INSTANT

When you are in "only human mode," you see life through a very narrow lens. There is limited flexibility in your point of view. Stuck in the drama, you don't make the critical shift beyond the story to find a higher perspective.

When you, the soul, leave your physical body behind, you will have no choice but to broaden your perspective. Shortly upon your arrival in the nonphysical realms, you will experience a reenactment of your human role in Earth School, as if viewing a movie. This is commonly referred to as "the life review."

During this experience, you will feel the effects of your interactions with others from their point of view. Their feelings become yours. From this alternate perspective, you gain greater understanding of the choices you made and their far-reaching effects.

Why wait until you die to have this eye-opening experience? As a projection of Consciousness, you are not limited to seeing only through your unique human window on the world. Awareness is malleable. Your thoughts and actions can change in an instant with the understanding that comes from seeing through another's eyes.

Point of view is everything.

I once did a session with a woman in my community whose deceased mother appeared very clearly in my mind's eye. She approached me with her head bowed. "Your mother is here with an apology," I announced, and immediately, my client stiffened.

Clearly, my statement had struck a sensitive spot, so I silently asked the mother to provide details. Instead of speaking, the older woman made a motion of cradling a baby and then mimed tossing that baby over her shoulder.

"Your mother says she is sorry for abandoning you as a child," I reported.

"Yeah. Me and my seven brothers and sisters," my client replied with a bitter tone.

I silently asked the mother if she had more to share. She immediately filled my mind with details of the challenging circumstances that led her to leave her family. My client listened with her head tilted to one side. It appeared that this was the first time she had set aside her own pain and considered her mother's suffering.

At the end of our session, my client rose from her chair and began to leave. She paused in the doorway, turned back to face me, and said, "I want you to know I have carried anger at my mother for 75 years, and in less than an hour, it has completely disappeared."

The hard lines around the woman's mouth softened before my eyes. Her face had a glow that was not there earlier.

Resentment and anger can last for a lifetime when you remain stuck in human mode. Forgiveness only takes an instant when you step outside the story and gain the soul's perspective.

When you harbor anger or blame toward another or yourself, you run that painful story over and over in your head. Forgiveness brings closure by cutting the cord that is holding *you* prisoner.

By saying, "I forgive this situation," you are not condoning what happened. You are not labeling it right or wrong. You are releasing the issue to the Universe. It no longer hangs over you like a dark cloud, dampening your own light.

Hurt people hurt people. This understanding can free you. It is the ego that holds on to stories that stunt your spiritual growth. Uplevel to the soul's perspective and see with new eyes. Uplevel yet again and know that no matter what, at the deepest level far beyond the story, all is well.

Poem #132 from The Council of Poets

Forgiveness is the greatest gift

When used to heal a painful rift.

Those who harbor pain and anger,

Who hold for others hardened rancor,

Hold within their chest a stone

Leaving them to feel alone.

Yet when you find it in your heart

To heal what sets you apart,

Then you know the inner peace

That enters with a great release.

It comes when you can finally say,

"I do forgive you on this day."

Forgiveness doesn't say, "You're right."

It doesn't carry power and might.

It's nothing but a touch of grace

That brushes softly 'cross the face.

And without judgment says, "I know

That all of us are here to grow.

And if I send you love, not hate,

Then easier will be your fate."

For all must pay for what they do.

You face your actions, this is true.

But seeing that all do err

And showing that the love's still there

Then in this way you show to all

That even those who take a fall

Can walk the straight and narrow path

When met with love instead of wrath.

REWRITING YOUR PAST ENERGETICALLY

Time is one of the givens of life in physical form that differentiates normal waking human consciousness from other states of being. While in Earth School, you experience the unfolding of events moving like an arrow from past to present to future.

Time is one of the variables that makes the earthly realm such an excellent learning environment. When you make choices in this dimension, you don't always see the results immediately. Cause and effect are not instantaneous like they are in the nonphysical domains. This delay in reaping what you sow may cause you to think that events in your life are random, chaotic, or even unjust. Often you can only see the connection when you shift to a higher perspective.

Happily, as Aware Awareness, you are not limited to the physical reality. With intention, you can shift to other states where there is only the eternal "now." If timelessness seems hard to imagine, think about your experiences while dreaming. All events occur without any sense of time passing.

Once you accept that the greater part of you transcends time and space, you can use this awareness to heal emotional wounds, no matter when they occurred.

Your past experiences exist for all eternity in the Sea of Consciousness. They are patterns of energy, and as you know, energy cannot be destroyed. However, most important for the purposes of healing, energy can most definitely be transformed.

To turn your scars into glowworms, recall an event from the past that continues to affect you negatively. Imagine how your life would be today if that event had unfolded differently. Envision how empowered you would be if you had known then what you know now. Imagine if you could rewrite this part of your story.

You can.

Athletes know the value of visualization. They use it effectively to prepare for sporting events that have not yet happened. By using the power of Consciousness to create their desired performance, they experience themselves performing at higher levels during the actual event. Creative visualization has the same effect when you reverse the arrow of time.

Understand that in this limited reality, there are restrictions as to what aspects of the past you can affect. The rules of Earth School say that you can't change the physical circumstances in your human history because these are part of a shared reality co-created with other beings. You can, however, relive any past event and change your mental and emotional reactions to it.

This is the difference between the outer, objective world and the inner, subjective reality. Your inner world exists outside of time. Consequently, any changes that you make to your past thoughts and emotions carry over to your energetic field in the present.

To rewrite your past energetically:

- Choose an event you would like to heal.

- Set aside a time and space where you won't be interrupted.

- Choose a preferred process, such as The
  BLESS ME Method, and enter into a state of
  expanded consciousness.

- Once your body is relaxed and your mind
  is focused and alert, shift to soul awareness.
  Affirm that you are ready and willing to
  review the chosen event from a neutral and
  compassionate perspective.

- Invite any helpful subtle beings to hold sacred
  space and guide you as you go through this
  healing process.

- Bring the specific event you have chosen
  into awareness. Review it frame by frame as
  if watching a movie. Hold the intention to
  remain detached and loving toward all souls
  involved, including the role you played at
  that time in your human story.

- See and understand what caused any others
  in this scenario to speak and act the way they
  did at the time.

- In awareness of how you reacted when the
  event unfolded in the physical world, rewrite
  your part of the story. Relive your thoughts
  and emotions completely anew from the
  empowered perspective of Aware Awareness
  that is always whole and cannot be harmed.

- Allow yourself to fully feel and own the
  higher vibrations that now honor yourself
  and all involved with greater understanding
  and compassion.

- Affirm that your vision is the new reality of this event within your soul's energy field.

- Send a wave of gratitude to the Universe for the healing that has taken place as a result of your efforts.

- Return to normal waking consciousness.

This is a powerful practice. You may notice immediate changes, such as feelings of lightness and relief. Other beneficial behaviors more aligned with the soul will reveal themselves over time.

Time . . . is no longer your adversary but a tool for transformation.

CONCLUSION

Transformation. Considering that the purpose of life in human form is to experience the richness of all that is, the word *transformation* may seem paradoxical. If you're here for the fullness, which includes happiness, sadness, joy, fear, grief, loss, pain, and gain, then why bother to change anything?

You are drawn to transformation because of the creative urge that naturally bubbles up within you moment by moment. At your deepest level, you are this Creative Intelligence. You came here to use your creative powers to learn and grow and to transform all experiences by leaving sparkles of your luminescence on all that you touch.

It is the very fullness of experience with all its ups and downs that brings about your transformation.

An empty container is transformed by a change of state into fullness. A full container, when emptied, has simply been transformed to what is part of its natural state of being. A full container and an empty container are not separate but are interdependent entities. Emptiness and fullness cannot exist without the other. What unites and reconciles the two is unchanging and ever-present . . . it is Wholeness.

In the process of awakening to your true nature, you realize that the emptiness you once fled from has been transformed by shining the light of Awareness onto it. You may continue to feel empty at times, but you now know this as a temporary condition that serves the purpose of nudging you back to Wholeness. In This-Awareness, you experience a fullness that cannot be contained.

You know this state now as Love . . . not the fleeting kind of love with human have-tos and shoulds imposed upon it, but that which has always been right here inside you . . . the unconditional kind that says, "You are so very loved . . . no matter what."

This is the promise and the guarantee of 21st-century spirituality and living The Awakened Way.

In the past you may have felt lost. You may well have such moments in the future when the drama of the human world draws you in again. But you know now that past and future are elements of the human story. In This-Awareness, you make the all-important, all-powerful *shift* beyond the story and find Joy here and now. You no longer seek to escape from the story. You see it for what it is: part of your Wholeness.

Through Self-Realization, you recognize that life in human form comes with challenges that you previously labeled "problems." The only problem worth resolving is the sense of a separate "me." In the awareness of your multi-dimensional nature as Aware Awareness in expression, all other problems are transformed into opportunities. You know with all certainty that at the deepest level, all is well.

Committed to remaining awake and aware, you are snagged by moments of misalignment. You stop, *shift*, and ask:

- What thoughts are causing this discomfort?

- Why am I hitting a wall within my human role? What is the Higher Self trying to communicate?

- What point of view am I living from? Am I stuck in "only human" mode or could I uplevel to a higher perspective?

- Who's in charge here, ego, Soul, or Joy?

The seeking is over. You live each moment consciously connected and divinely guided, allowing life to unfold, taking appropriate action as guided from the heart. Inspired responses arise as you remain attuned to the Creative Intelligence within.

In This-Awareness, "The Story of You" is transformed, for you realize that there is ultimately only One Story, and you know it as Love in Full Expression.

This greater, never-ending narrative is an anthology filled to overflowing with stories within stories. As you move forward in time and beyond time, you finally, gratefully remember once again that you are the author, the protagonist, and all other characters fully fleshed out.

And you know that you are also the Reader who simply can't put the book down. It's a page-turner, this Story of LIFE, and you are all-in.

APPENDIX

Helpful Resources

What follows is a treasury of tools to accompany the teaching and exercises shared in this book to further your Awakened Way journey.

THE AWAKENED WAY APP

Available for IOS and Android users, this free app provides a wealth of resources at your fingertips, including the Daily Way messages delivered from Suzanne's guides in spirit and the meditations listed below. Search for "Awakened Way" in the App Store or Google Play. See more information at: https://suzannegiesemann.com/awakenedwayapp

AUTHOR WEBSITE

Find all the latest resources to guide you along The Awakened Way.

https://suzannegiesemann.com

FREE RESOURCES

E-Books:

MASTERING MEDITATION:
An e-book filled with advice from Suzanne's guides in spirit and her many tools to help you get started with or expand your meditation practice. https://suzannegiesemann.com/books/e-booklet-mastering-meditation

Meditations:

Note: Video and audio links to the following meditations can be found at: https://suzannegiesemann.com/gifts-to-help-you-connect-with-spirit

BLESS ME METHOD: A memory device and process to use with any meditation.

"I AM" MEDITATION: Go directly to Source.

SIP OF THE DIVINE: Three minutes to find peace and answers.

THE 10-MINUTE TRANSFORMATION: Chakra clearing and balancing.

THE JOURNEY OF REMEMBRANCE: A channeled meditation to walk you through the seven innate aspects of who you are.

THE JOURNEY OF CONSCIOUSNESS: A channeled meditation to lead you to the memory of who you really are.

MAKING THE CONNECTION: A 20-minute session to connect with Higher Consciousness.

POWERFUL NEW YEAR MEDITATION: Use this meditation to see your human role from the soul's perspective and upgrade to a higher version of your greatest self.

RADIANT HEART: A meditation from the book *Wolf's Message* that takes you to a state of peace and balance.

RECORDED WORKSHOPS

HEART GIFTS: Experience the story of Wolf, the young man in spirit who was introduced in "The Soul Knows" section of this book. The story of his communication with Suzanne has been described as a "masterpiece of intrigue." Learn the profound messages he has for humanity. https://youtu.be/zJeLPy22feI

AWAKENED LIVING: A workshop to provide essential tools for thriving as a fully conscious transdimensional being. Find greater joy, peace, and a connection with all that is. https://youtu.be/SkwvSfCJvvM

VIDEOS

IRENE'S HEALING: See Irene and hear the firsthand account of an experience with Carly, her daughter on the other side, in this video clip from a conference presentation. https://youtu.be/6xzYzl3-n1I

SHE SPOKE TO A NORSE GOD: Enjoy watching this short video of Suzanne's evidential meeting with Odin as described in "All Is Not as It Seems" in this book. https://youtu.be/BTxUv5Cty60

POINT OF VIEW IS EVERYTHING: Review highlights of the discussion about points of view in this video clip. https://youtu.be/79qgE6AMbL0

HOW DO SPIRIT GUIDES COMMUNICATE WITH US? Learn more about the communication process and the creative ways spirit guides connect with us in this short video. https://youtu.be/oluKa7jA7q0

ANGELS ARE REAL—HOW ABOUT SOME EVIDENCE: Hear two true stories in this short video clip with more evidence that we are never alone. https://youtu.be/7yYlN-Rg0zk

I AM THIS: Listen to a profound answer to "Who am I?" as given by guides on the other side who call themselves Sanaya. https://youtu.be/vJupQzoMA34

OCEAN BREATHING: Watch a video describing Ocean Breathing, as shared in "Getting to Know Your True Nature." https://youtu.be/ZClp7evfjr8

A TOOL TO SEE THE ONENESS: This video clip demonstrates the powerful mala bead exercise shared in the "Joy-Us Beads" Exercise in Section 1 of Part II. https://youtu.be/GxOFA7rERdQ

DO WE NEED TO REMEMBER WHO WE ARE? An answer comes directly from the spirit realm in this short video clip from a *Messages of Hope* podcast. https://youtu.be/ahEe8UtYACU

BACK TO BALANCE: See the Crossbar Technique and practice using this powerful tool. https://youtu.be/ITZaeL4ixWU

NO FAULT PROCESS: See the seven-step process given to Suzanne by her teachers in Spirit to change unhealthy reactions to a state of peace and wholeness. https://youtu.be/mt0BmG7sas4

ADDITIONAL RESOURCES

RECORDINGS

https://suzannegiesemann.com/hemi-sync-tools-for-awakening-series

GETTING TO KNOW YOUR TRUE NATURE: Hemi-Sync recording with tones and words to take you to unconditional love and peace as a soul.

YOU BEYOND YOUR STORY: Hemi-Sync recording with tones and words to shift from the narrow human story to experience a state of wholeness.

BOOKS

MESSAGES OF HOPE: Suzanne's story of how she made the transition from Navy Commander to her current work. Filled with evidence of the greater reality, it opens readers to awareness of our multidimensional nature.

WOLF'S MESSAGE: Described as a "masterpiece of intrigue," this nonfiction book tells the story of the young man nicknamed Wolf.

LOVE BEYOND WORDS & IN THE SILENCE: Each volume contains one year's worth of inspirational and informational messages from Suzanne's guides in spirit, Sanaya.

ACKNOWLEDGMENTS

The way this book came to be is a reflection of the three main principles of The Awakened Way:

1. You are not only human. This I know thanks to the magnificent beings in the nonphysical realms who have shared their love and wisdom and helped me come to know who we really are. They tell me there is no hierarchy across the veil, but I bow in humility and gratitude to the expressions of Source known as Susan, Wolf, Brenda, Carly, Boris, Michael, Jesus, Odin, Sanaya, and any other unseen beings I may not have recognized.

2. You are part of one big web connecting all that is. I give thanks each day for the web of relationships in my life that bring such joy and allow us to spread ripples of love throughout the world. I could not do this work without the unconditional love and support of my soulmate, Ty, and the best team of earthly helpers I could ask for: Bev Garlipp, Lynette Setzkorn, Valerie Kwietniak, Jayesh Mitha, and Stephanie Pfennig. Thank you for always going "above and beyond" for me and for Spirit. You all played an integral role in bringing this book to fruition.

Much gratitude to Lee Lawrence for your insights over the years and for allowing me to share what I call "The Crossbar Technique." Diane Ray at MindBodySpirit.FM, I am indebted to you for saying "yes." Amy Kiberd and Sally Mason-Swaab at Hay House, thank you for believing in me and my work and for shepherding these words from manuscript to book in print. Irene and Tony Vouvalides, Mike and Beth Pasakarnis, I treasure our friendship. Our children in spirit brought us together through the web and the experiences we have shared continue to let others know that love never dies.

3. The healing and creative force of the Universe is Love. I feel the love each day from you, the members of this beautiful Awakened Way community. Together, as we make the shift to a divinely guided life, we are healing ourselves and each other, creating a brighter world for all beings everywhere.

ABOUT THE AUTHOR

Spiritual teacher and medium **Suzanne Giesemann** knows how to live in a left-brained world. As a U.S. Navy commander and aide to the head of the U.S. military on 9/11, she was unaware of anything beyond this earthly realm. The death of her pregnant stepdaughter by lightning strike catapulted Suzanne on a journey that led to the unexpected gift of evidence-based communication with nonphysical Consciousness.

Known for her joyful, down-to-earth style and making deep spiritual concepts easy to understand, Suzanne laces her teaching with evidence-filled stories of the greater reality and practical tools that provide proof of our multi-dimensional nature.

She has authored numerous books, six best-selling Hemi-Sync recordings, and YouTube videos reaching over nine million viewers. She produces the Awakened Way app with daily inspirational messages and hosts the top-ranking *Messages of Hope* podcast. She leads classes, workshops, and retreats in person and online to help people make the shift to a divinely guided life.

Website: **suzannegiesemann.com**

Hay House Titles of Related Interest

YOU CAN HEAL YOUR LIFE, the movie,
starring Louise Hay & Friends
(available as an online streaming video)
www.hayhouse.com/louise-movie

THE SHIFT, the movie,
starring Dr. Wayne W. Dyer
(available as an online streaming video)
www.hayhouse.com/the-shift-movie

***

*21 DAYS TO JUMP-START YOUR INTUITION: Awaken Your Most
Empowering Super Sense,* by Sonia Choquette

A TIME FOR GRACE: Sacred Guidance for Everyday Life, by
Caroline Myss

*THE WISDOM CODES: Ancient Words to Rewire Our Brains and
Heal Our Hearts,* by Gregg Braden

*WISDOM FROM YOUR SPIRIT GUIDES: A Handbook to Contact
Your Soul's Greatest Teachers,* by James Van Praagh

All of the above are available at www.hayhouse.co.uk.

***

CONNECT WITH
HAY HOUSE
ONLINE

🌐 hayhouse.co.uk   **f** @hayhouse

📷 @hayhouseuk   **X** @hayhouseuk

▶ @hayhouseuk   ♪ @hayhouseuk

Find out all about our latest books & card decks • Be the first
to know about exclusive discounts • Interact with our authors
in live broadcasts • Celebrate the cycle of the seasons with us
• Watch free videos from your favourite authors •
Connect with like-minded souls

*'The gateways to wisdom and knowledge
are always open.'*

Louise Hay